T0397285

Leadership Development in Public Relations

Through interviews with members of the Public Relations Society of America College of Fellows, this book provides lessons on public relations leadership for the next generation.

Often, our focus on high-profile leaders is centered on success stories, but so much can be learned from the trials, or "crucibles," they have faced and how leaders overcame and were shaped by these challenges. The Fellows interviewed represent a diverse group of accomplished professionals with specializations ranging from military public affairs and government, corporate, education, agency, and nonprofit organizations. A focus on ethical values, virtues, and ethical leadership will inspire readers to themselves confidently lead.

This book will be of interest to advanced students in public relations programs or young professionals looking to forge their careers in public relations leadership.

Marlene S. Neill is an associate professor and graduate program director at Baylor University, USA.

Routledge Research in Public Relations

Bringing together theories and thought from a variety of perspectives, this series features cutting-edge research addressing all the major issues in public relations today, helping to define and advance the field.

5 **Public Relations and Religion in American History**
Evangelism, Temperance, and Businessd
Margot Opdycke Lamme

8 **The Moral Compass of Public Relations**
Edited by Brigitta R. Brunner

9 **Relationship Building in Public Relations**
Petra Theunissen and Helen Sissons

10 **Advancing Crisis Communication Effectiveness**
Integrating Public Relations Scholarship with Practice
Edited by Yan Jin, Bryan H. Reber, and Glen J. Nowak

11 **Internal Communication and Employer Brands**
Ana Tkalac Verčič, Dejan Verčič, and Anja Špoljarić

12 **Organizational Listening for Strategic Communication**
Building Theory and Practice
Katie R. Place

13 **Leadership Development in Public Relations**
Exploring Crucibles of Experience Among Industry Veterans
Marlene S. Neill

For more information about this series, please visit: www.routledge.com/Routledge-Research-in-Public-Relations/book-series/RRPR

Leadership Development in Public Relations

Exploring Crucibles of Experience Among Industry Veterans

Marlene S. Neill

Routledge
Taylor & Francis Group
NEW YORK AND LONDON

First published 2024
by Routledge
605 Third Avenue, New York, NY 10158

and by Routledge
4 Park Square, Milton Park, Abingdon, Oxon, OX14 4RN

Routledge is an imprint of the Taylor & Francis Group, an informa business

ISBN: 978-103-2-58840-7 (hbk)
ISBN: 978-103-2-58839-1 (pbk)
ISBN: 978-100-3-45170-9 (ebk)

DOI: 10.4324/9781003451709

Typeset in Times New Roman
by Apex CoVantage, LLC

I would like to dedicate this book to my husband, Terry, and early-career mentors, Gene Hall and Blake Lewis, whose personal stories are included in this book.

Contents

Foreword   *viii*
DENISE SEVICK BORTREE
Foreword   *x*
MARGARET ANN HENNEN
Acknowledgments   *xii*

1 Crucibles, Leader Development, and Narratives   1

2 The Participants and History of the PRSA College of Fellows   11

3 Development of Identity   25

4 Crucible Experiences   36

5 Critical Reflection   57

6 Phronesis – Practical Wisdom and Resilience   70

7 Ethical Leadership   85

8 Conclusion: The Future of Ethical Leadership   101

Appendix A: Biographies   *110*
Index   *125*

Foreword

The Arthur W. Page Center for Integrity in Public Communication is pleased to be a sponsor for the research work in this cutting-edge book. Through interviews conducted with members of the Public Relations Society of America's College of Fellows, Drs. Marlene Neill and Katie Place draw out the meaningful experiences that have formed the values and beliefs of some of the most prominent leaders in the public relations space. This book makes a meaningful contribution to our understanding of good leadership in the public relations and communication industries.

How are great leadership skills developed? Is there a formula for becoming a great leader and an ethical decision-maker? And, what can young communication professionals do to build ethical leadership skills? These are fascinating questions, and Neill's book offers useful insights. Her research suggests that each leader takes a different path with some commonalities. In short, what seems to create moral and ethical leaders is the way they embrace and respond to trials in their lives. They are resilient. They face challenges and demonstrate moral courage . . . most of the time. But, it's messy sometimes. This book isn't a roadmap to success but rather a reflection on how leadership evolves over time, and that makes the findings particularly appealing.

Today's media landscape is fraught with issues due in part to the proliferation of disinformation and bad actors. What the communication fields need are leaders who will take a stand for truth, transparency, and respect for stakeholders. This book helps us understand how some of the leading professionals and scholars arrived at a place where they are willing to advocate for integrity in communication. This is useful for current leaders and also for upcoming professionals and scholars.

As the next generation faces a new set of challenges, they can learn from the experience of the leaders interviewed for this book. The themes and lessons learned that emerge offer hope to young people who are currently facing challenges in their lives. Maybe these trials are the crucible experiences that will stimulate growth and provide practical wisdom needed in future leadership roles. Embrace them. As Neill encourages in her final chapter, ongoing ethical education and training is key to life-long learning and development for good decision-making. As the communication space becomes more complex, we need leaders with a strong moral compass.

This book offers hope and inspiration. I hope you find it as fascinating as I did.

Denise Sevick Bortree, Ph.D.
Director, The Arthur W. Page Center for Integrity
in Public Communication
Professor and Associate Dean, Bellisario College
of Communications, Penn State University

Foreword

This book combines Marlene Neill's well known, direct work on ethical public relations and her insightful work on leadership development. Her approach to ethics and exemplary public relations underscores her commitment to leadership, ethics, and those who lead by example to ensure the strength of our profession. She encourages introspection on our careers, our leadership, and our future, no matter where we are in our lives.

The book fills a gap in the public relations story as it shares the leadership development of 40 individuals who are prominent in the profession in the twenty-first century. Through her primary qualitative research, Marlene Neill illustrates how life lessons of 40 members of the PRSA College of Fellows correlate with her secondary research on the characteristics and development of outstanding leaders. The stories these leaders shared will attract fellow public relations professionals currently practicing and teaching in the profession. In addition, the coupling of theory and practical life experience will inspire students and emerging public relations professionals who aspire to follow in advancing and leading the profession into the future.

The path to ethical public relations leadership for each of those interviewed shows some of the diverse experiences and achievements which formed these exemplary leaders. It looks at lessons learned and resilience gained to overcome disappointment or failure and to celebrate success.

The College of Fellows is comprised of professionals who have earned accreditation in public relations (APR), who have at least 20 years of experience practicing or teaching public relations, and who have demonstrated exemplary public relations performance. Each shares a footprint of work that helps form the Body of Knowledge required for any field to claim professionalism and to strive for excellence. This footprint varies from person to person but frequently reflects best-practice breakthrough methods, research, and new Community Standards for performance, etc.

A gifted writer and interviewer, Neill has gained the trust of many, including those she interviewed, over a couple decades working together on PRSA committees and projects. As a result, the leadership of the College of Fellows readily gave Neill its endorsement and consulted with her throughout the process of creating this book. The College of Fellows thanks Marlene Neill for preserving the stories of these stalwarts of our profession in their own words and giving them a public voice. This work is undertaken in conjunction with Baylor University, where the full interviews will be archived for future research.

In her final chapter, Neill lifts the curtain on some of what lies ahead for our profession and members of the College.

Margaret Ann Hennen, APR, Fellow PRSA
2022 Chair of the PRSA College of Fellows

Acknowledgments

A project of this scale is only possible through the support and contributions of many individuals and organizations who support public relations leadership and preservation of oral history research, and I am grateful for their support. First of all, thank you to the Arthur W. Page Center for Integrity in Public Communication at Penn State University and the Baylor University Institute for Oral History for sponsoring and funding this research project and for providing technical support related to the transcription and historical preservation of audio, video, and photos compiled for this study. Thank you to the leadership of the PRSA College of Fellows for their support throughout the two-year study and to the 40 Fellows who participated in the interviews and were willing to openly share their personal stories. Thank you to Katie R. Place for assisting with the interview phase of the project. I also would like to express my appreciation to Felisa Salvago-Keyes and Sean Daley at Routledge for their support throughout the proposal and production process. I would also like to thank Patrick L. Plaisance, who introduced me to the life story interview process and served as the inspiration for this project. Finally, thank you to my employer Baylor University and Department Chair Dr. Mia Moody-Ramirez for supporting academic research studies such as this one.

Marlene S. Neill

1 Crucibles, Leader Development, and Narratives

Introduction

Imagine the wisdom that can be gleaned by sitting down with 40 diverse public relations leaders and asking them to share their life stories. We did just that – spending about two hours, on average, listening to each of their stories. Those stories were then transcribed and archived for historical and research purposes through a partnership with the Baylor University Institute for Oral History.[1] A book containing their full accounts would be quite lengthy and overwhelming, so highlights have been selected from their stories that illustrate life lessons for young professionals who aspire to follow in their footsteps as leaders. Specifically, we asked these leaders to recall moments of trials, referred to as crucibles, and how those experiences shaped their values and the way they lead. Bennis and Thomas (2006) described a crucible experience as a "trial and test, a point of deep self-reflection that forces them [leaders] to examine their values, question their assumptions, and hone their judgment" (p. 15). Other scholars have referred to these experiences as trigger events, and whether the experiences are positive or negative, they can result in leader development (Gardner et al., 2005; Shannon et al., 2020). Historically, a crucible referred to a vessel that was used in the refining process while heating metals to remove impurities and create gold (Bennis & Thomas, 2006).

These crucible moments are so impactful in the lives of each leader that he or she often "creates a narrative" (i.e., a story) that communicates exactly "how he or she was challenged, met that challenge, and became a new and better self " (Bennis & Thomas, 2002, p. 108). Thomas (2009) classified crucible experiences into three primary categories: *new territory*, which "sharpen an individual's alertness to new information and his or her skill at sense-making"; *reversal*, which includes experiences such as the death of a

1 The full transcripts, videos, audio, and photographs will be archived at: https://library.web.baylor.edu/oralhistory

DOI: 10.4324/9781003451709-1

loved one, health issues, divorce, financial difficulty, or failure in a major task or assignment; and *suspension*, which refers to experiences that challenge leaders to "clarify – or . . . to create – their personal mission and purpose; to cement their own personal foundation of beliefs and values" (pp. 21, 25). Bennis and Thomas (2002) pointed out that crucibles can end in failure – as emerging leaders do not know in the midst of the crucible "how the story is going to end or what [their] fate is going to be" (p. 100). Crucibles can also include an *encounter* or *identity crisis* (Cross, 1978; Erikson, 1968), such as confronting discrimination, which can result in confidence and the ability to deflect the negativity (Oetzel, 2009). In fact, all of these types of experiences (i.e., new territory, reversals, and suspension) are discussed throughout this book and how they shaped the Fellows we interviewed.

It is important to note that in Chance's study (2021), which focused on crucible experiences of Black women leaders working in higher education, she found they experienced "compounded adversities" including "physical, sexual, and verbal assault and abuse, adverse childhood experiences such as growing up in poverty, being raised by single parents, being subject to bullying, losing loved ones, discrimination, and health issues" (p. 601). These findings provide support for the importance of studying crucibles faced by diverse leaders, which will be addressed more in Chapter 3. Chance (2021) concluded that Black women leaders were able to overcome these barriers through resilience. In his study of crucibles faced by exemplars in the media industry, Plaisance (2015) characterized their resilience as the "ability to cope effectively and not be debilitated by adversity or hardship, the ability to perceive benefits derived from difficult experiences, the ability to respond to harsh realities with flexibility and adaptation rather than with bitterness and belligerence" (p. 183). Buzzanell (2010) listed five approaches associated with achieving resiliency:

(a) crafting normalcy (e.g., maintaining the mundane or routine activities), (b) affirming identity anchors (e.g., religion, spirituality), (c) maintaining and using communication networks, (d) putting alternative logics to work (i.e., reframing the situation), and (e) downplaying negative feelings while foregrounding positive emotions, such as hopefulness and self-efficacy.

(p. 1)

Indeed, readers will recognize some of these approaches as applied by the public relations leaders we interviewed, as they recall their own crucibles and how they overcame them.

Life Story Interview

For this study, we used an interview guide created by McAdams, which was developed for a specific type of in-depth interview called "life stories." The guide is based on his beliefs as a psychologist that the development of personal identity, which encompasses someone's purpose in life and values, "takes the form of a story, complete with setting, scenes, character, plot, and theme" (McAdams, 2001, p. 101). The guide begins with participants discussing their lives in the form of a book and identifying the various life chapters. They then discuss key scenes in their lives such as a high point, low point, turning point, and wisdom event. Some of these experiences do involve crucibles. The participants are then asked about their future plans and goals. As McAdams (2001) pointed out:

> We choose the events that we consider most important for defining who we are and providing our lives with some semblance of unity and purpose. And we endow them with symbolic messages, lessons learned, integrative themes, and other personal meanings that make sense to us in the present as we survey the past and anticipate the future.
>
> (p. 110)

The guide next involves a discussion on life challenges including a failure or regret. They then discuss their personal ideology including religious and ethical values, their personal development (e.g., role model, college experience), a personal virtue, a personal vice, and life theme. In support of this approach, Gardner et al. (2005) suggested that personal history is a critical component of leader development, which would include family, childhood, education, work history, role models, and earlier leadership experiences.

McAdams (2001) pointed out that some memories are "especially vivid or consequential" to one's self-identity, such as *memorable messages* or those that serve as a "guiding statement or moral directive"; *symbolic messages* impart "implicit lessons or guidelines"; *originating events* symbolize the "genesis of an interest, vocation, relations, life goal"; *anchoring events* are those that "affirm and reinforce an ongoing interest, attitude or commitment"; and *analogous events* evoke a pattern or theme that runs throughout the individual's life (Pillemer, 1998; p. 109). In fact, specific examples of these types of experiences are shared, as recalled by the public relations leaders that we interviewed, as well as what made these moments so impactful and the lessons they gleaned.

McAdams and his colleagues (1996) also examine life stories for specific themes. Of particular interest are those focused on *agency* (e.g., self-mastery, status, achievement/responsibility and empowerment) and *communion* (e.g., love/ friendship, dialogue, care/help, and community). These themes tend to emerge when participants are discussing emotionally positive scenes and turning points as well as memories associated with both adolescence and adulthood (McAdams et al., 1996). Under the category of *agency*, McAdams et al. (1996) explained:

> The person high in achievement motivation seeks to do well, be successful, and move steadily onward and upward into the future as an effective

and competent agent, meeting successive challenges, accomplishing successive goals, and building on successive achievements to create a bigger and better legacy of the self.

(pp. 347–348)

These characteristics associated with *achievement/ responsibility* are consistent with motivations discussed by members of the College of Fellows. Also consistent with *agency* is *empowerment*, which is

manifested in accounts in which the individual is enlarged, enhanced, empowered, ennobled, built up, or made better through his or her association with an especially powerful source, such as God, nature, the universe, or some highly charismatic or inspiring figure.

(McAdams et al., 1996, p. 348)

Accounts that reflect empowerment are also included in the following chapters. While less common, there are some Fellows' narratives that are consistent with the themes associated with *communion* or expressions of "altruism, sympathy, care, and helping others in need" (McAdams et al., 1996, p. 350). The specific narratives may mention persons in trouble; those who need help; children, students or young professionals they mentor; charitable organizations; and even how we treat others in general, such as by demonstrating empathy or kindness (McAdams et al., 1996). These accounts are discussed in Chapters 6, 7, and 8, which are focused on wisdom and ethical leadership.

Role of Crucibles in Leader Development

At this point, it is appropriate to introduce a framework that depicts the journey public relations leaders completed when developing their personal identities over a lifetime (see Figure 1.2). I approached this study with the core belief that leaders can acquire and develop essential skills and capabilities through personal experiences and training rather than simply being a trait they possess at birth (Northouse, 2018). *Leader development* refers to "individual growth and skill advancement" and is the focus of this book with the hope that the Fellows' stories will inspire the next generation of leaders (Berger & Meng, 2014, p. 32). In comparison, *leadership development* refers to an organization's "planned attempts and programs to systematically develop its leadership team over time" (Berger & Meng, 2014, p. 32).

It is also important to point out that not all of the leaders we interviewed had idealistic childhoods that would be expected to set someone up for career success (Colby & Damon, 1992). In fact, some grew up in poverty. One participant in our study lost his father at a young age, and another participant was raised by her grandmother and aunts, which illustrates that exemplars learn and grow from their own unique personal experiences, including crucibles (Colby & Damon, 1992). Throughout their lifetimes, these public relations leaders have faced a number of crucibles that have shaped them and the way they lead, which they will describe in detail in Chapter 4. However, to actually discover lessons from those experiences, they had to take time for critical reflection, which involves examining "who they are at their very core, understanding where they stand with regard to their character strengths and weaknesses" (Byrne et al., 2018, p. 268; see Sidebar). Chapter 5 will delve more into the experience of critical reflection among our participants with particular attention focused on life challenges, low points, turning points, failures, and regrets. This experience is not always a pleasant one, especially following circumstances when a leader realizes that he or she did not live up to his or her ideals or values (Byrne et al., 2018). Kernis (2003) emphasized the importance of engaging in unbiased processing, which means "not denying, distorting, exaggerating, or ignoring private knowledge, internal experiences, and externally based evaluative information. Instead, it involves objectivity and acceptance of one's positive and negative aspects, attributes, and qualities" (p. 14). Following a time of critical reflection, the crucible experience then becomes that "tipping point" when "new identities are weighed, where values are examined and strengthened or replaced, and where one's judgment and other abilities are honed" (Bennis & Thomas, 2002, p. 106).

Fred Cook, Fellow PRSA, Chair Emeritus at Golin, said that he engaged in critical reflection when writing his memoirs, which resulted in him writing a career advice book titled, "Improvise: Unconventional Career Advice from an Unlikely CEO." He discussed the value of this practice:

> I think it's a good exercise for anybody to write down what they've done in their life and look back on it and think, what have I learned from this? Because you don't know at the time what you're learning – you can't see it as it's happening – but when you look back, you begin to see those threads, and you begin to see the things that pop out that weren't obvious at the time.

Figure 1.1   Fred Cook with Al Golin, the co-founder of Golin/Harris. Cook eventually became the CEO of this global agency.

Figure 1.2 Impact of crucibles on leader development (Neill & Meng, 2022).

These experiences then result in the development of their personal character and virtues. In support of this theory, Bennis and Thomas (2002) previously detected several leadership proficiencies and virtues that were cultivated through the experience of various crucibles, such as adaptive capacity (i.e., problem solving), creativity, empathy, self-awareness, emotional intelligence, and integrity. Some of these competencies are consistent with those that are necessary for excellent leadership in public relations, such as strategic decision making, the ability to solve problems, relationship building, and ethical values and orientation (Meng et al., 2012). An ethical orientation in the context of public relations leadership has been described as "the extent to which public relations leaders believe in and enact professional values and standards when ethical and legal dilemmas arise and responsibilities and loyalties conflict" (Meng & Berger, 2013, p. 148; Bowen, 2004; Heath & Bowen, 2002; see Sidebar).

Michelle Egan is the 2023 national chair of the Public Relations Society of America (PRSA). She has made ethics one of her top priorities:

> We just finished a new strategic plan, guided by this North Star: we are a community of ethical communications professionals building for tomorrow, today. I believe *how* we do our work is just as important as the tasks we perform. All PRSA members agree to adhere to a strong Code of Ethics, and it's one of the things members value most about the organization. My goal for this year is to elevate as much as I can the importance of ethics in our profession, shining a light on our community and advocating for better practices everywhere.

Figure 1.3 Michelle Egan is the 2023 Chair of the Public Relations Society of America.

Regarding the ethical or moral development of leaders, a virtue or *habitus* is defined as a "predictable disposition to choose the good whenever confronted with a choice" (Pellegrino, 1995, p. 257). Through life story interviews with a group of leaders, Hemingway and Starkey (2018) concluded that crucibles "do provide the impetus to reframing one's values and acting accordingly" and that once virtues are triggered, they can become a constant component of that leader's character (p. 887). "When fully developed, virtues are habitual dispositions to choose right action through the exercise of practical reason, perfected by what Aristotle called *phronesis*, or practical wisdom: the hard-won moral expertise that comes from experience and reflection" (Borden, 2019, p. 172). Previous survey research with mid- and senior-level public relations executives revealed the top sources for leader development were on-the-job experiences, individual initiative and desire, examples set by role models, and powerful personal experiences and events (e.g., crucibles) (Meng et al., 2012). This will be the focus of Chapter 6 – Phronesis (i.e., Practical Wisdom) and Resilience.

We were motivated to specifically interview members of the Public Relations Society of America (PRSA) College of Fellows for this study due to their position as role models. In fact, it is core to the mission of the College of Fellows, and one of their primary service activities is providing a formal mentorship program. A discussion regarding the history of the College of Fellows is provided in Chapter 2, along with more information about the study participants. As Kelly Davis, a member of the 2020 class of inductees explained,

> One thing I love about the College is that they say . . . College of Fellows is not like . . . you get there and you're done . . . it is continued service and continued mentoring. And, you know, my friend Philip Tate is sort of credited with saying . . . "mentoring is the calling card of the College of Fellows. And so, when you reach the College of Fellows, it's not okay, check the box. I'm done. It's what is the next thing? What is the next level of service that I'm going to provide to the profession?"

Only 2% of the PRSA membership has achieved Fellow status, and they are widely esteemed for their ethical leadership and contributions to the discipline of public relations. The concept of ethical role models is central to virtue ethics. Baker (2008) wrote that "inherent to the virtue ethics perspective" is the responsibility of moral exemplars or role models who instruct others how to live moral lives (p. 239; Pojman, 2005). Through observing their lives and actively seeking counsel, protégés learn virtues or desirable character traits (Baker, 2008; Borden, 2019). For these reasons, Chapter 7 will focus on ethical leadership and specific examples of times when Fellows demonstrated moral courage as well as the virtues they live by.

Finally, I was interested in how the practical wisdom (i.e., *phronesis*) generated by these life experiences results in virtuous behaviors as leaders, which are observed by their employees and colleagues. Through this project, these leaders are asked to share their wisdom with an audience of young professionals who aspire to leadership roles. These lessons can best be communicated through the narratives as reconstructed by public relations leaders in their own words. Narratives are first-person accounts of personal experiences that are typically recounted in a story format with a beginning, middle, and end (Merriam, 2002). It's important for readers to pay attention to patterns or themes in their stories "by focusing on the way that individuals recount their histories – what they emphasize or leave out; their roles as heroes, villains, or victims in the plot; their self-talk; the way they talk about others" (Stern et al., 1998, p. 199).

The book will conclude with a chapter (Chapter 8) focused on the future of ethical leadership with practical implications and resources for young professionals who aspire to become leaders and recommendations for future research.

Questions to Consider

1. What are some examples of crucibles that you have faced in your life and what have you learned from the experiences?
2. Who would you consider to be a role model in your life and what is it that you admire about that person?

References

Baker, S. (2008). The model of the principled advocate and the pathological partisan: A virtue ethics construct of opposing archetypes of public relations and advertising practitioners. *Journal of Mass Media Ethics, 23*, 235–253.

Bennis, W. G., & Thomas, R. J. (2002). *Geeks and geezers: How era, values, and defining moments shape leaders*. Harvard Business School Publishing.

Bennis, W. G., & Thomas, R. J. (2006). Crucibles. *Leadership Excellence, 23*(7), 15.

Berger, B. K., & Meng, J. (Eds.). (2014). *Public relations leaders as sensemakers: A global study of leadership in public relations and communication management*. Routledge.

Borden, S. L. (2019). Virtue ethics & media. In P. L. Plaisance (Ed.), *Communication and media ethics* (pp. 171–190). Walter de Gruyter.

Bowen, S. A. (2004). Expansion of ethics as the tenth generic principle of public relations excellence: A Kantian theory and model for managing ethical issue. *Journal of Public Relations Research, 16*, 65–92.

Buzzanell, P. M. (2010). Resilience: Talking, resisting and imagining new normalcies into being. *Journal of Communication, 60*, 1–14.

Byrne, A., Crossan, M., & Seijts, G. (2018). The development of leader character through crucible moments. *Journal of Management Education, 42*(2), 265–293.

Chance, N. L. (2021). A phenomenological inquiry into the influence of crucible experiences on the leadership development of Black women in higher education senior leadership. *Educational Management Administration & Leadership, 49*(4), 601–623.

Colby, A., & Damon, W. (1992). *Some do care: Contemporary lives of moral commitment.* MacMillan, Inc.

Cross, W. (1978). The Thomas and cross models of psychological nigrescence: A literature review. *Journal of Black Psychology, 4,* 1331.

Erikson, E. (1968). *Identity: Youth and crisis.* Norton.

Gardner, W. L., Avolio, B. J., Luthans, F., May, D. R., & Walumbwa, F. (2005). "Can you see the real me?" A self-based model of authentic leader and follower development. *Leadership Quarterly, 16*(3), 343–372.

Heath, R. L., & Bowen, S. A. (2002). Public relations' role in defining corporate social responsibility. *Journal of Mass Media Ethics, 4*(1), 21–38.

Hemingway, C. A., & Starkey, K. (2018). A falling of the veils: Turning points and momentous turning points in leadership and the creation of CSR. *Journal of Business Ethics, 151,* 875–890.

Kernis, M. H. (2003). Toward a conceptualization of optimal self-esteem. *Psychological Inquiry, 14,* 1–26.

McAdams, D. P. (2001). The psychology of life stories. *Review of General Psychology, 5*(2), 100–122.

McAdams, D. P., Hoffman, B. J., Mansfield, E. D., & Day, R. (1996). Themes of agency and communion in significant autobiographical scenes. *Journal of Personality, 64*(2), 339–377.

Meng, J., & Berger, B. (2013). An integrated model of excellent leadership in public relations: Dimensions, measurement, and validation. *Journal of Public Relations Research, 25*(2), 141–167.

Meng, J., Berger, B., Gower, K., & Heyman, W. (2012). A test of excellent leadership in public relations: Key qualities, valuable sources, and distinctive leadership perceptions. *Journal of Public Relations Research, 24*(1), 18–36.

Merriam, S. B. (2002). *Qualitative research in practice: Examples for discussion and analysis.* Jossey-Bass.

Neill, M. S., & Meng, J. (2022). The impact of crucibles in developing public relations' character & competencies as servant leaders. *Journal of Media Ethics, 37*(3), 208–222.https://doi.org/10.1080/23736992.2022.2107526

Northouse, P. G. (2018). *Leadership: Theory and practice* (4th ed.). Sage.

Oetzel, J. G. (2009). *Intercultural communication: A layered approach.* Vanga Books.

Pellegrino, E. D. (1995). Toward a virtue-based normative ethics for the health professions. *Kennedy Institute of Ethics Journal, 5*(3), 252–277.

Pillemer, D. B. (1998). *Momentous events, vivid memories.* Harvard University Press.

Plaisance, P. L. (2015). *Virtue in media: The moral psychology of excellence in news and public relations.* Routledge.

Pojman, L. P. (2005). *How should we live? An introduction to ethics.* Thomson Wadsworth.

Shannon, M. R., Buford, M., Winston, B. E., & Wood, J. A. (2020). Trigger events and crucibles in authentic leaders' development. *Journal of Management Development, 39*(3), 324–333.

Stern, B. B., Thompson, C. J., & Arnould, E. J. (1998). Narrative analysis of a marketing relationship: The consumer's perspective. *Psychology & Marketing, 15*(3), 195–214.

Thomas, R. J. (2009). The leadership lessons of crucible experiences. *Journal of Business Strategy, 30*(1), 21–26.

2 The Participants and History of the PRSA College of Fellows

Introduction

We interviewed 40 members of the PRSA College of Fellows, most representing the Baby Boomers (born between 1946 and 1964) or Generation X (born between 1965 and 1980) and a few representing the Silent Generation (born between 1925 and 1945) (Dimock, 2019) (see Appendix for biographies). Unlike earlier publications focused on profiling the lives of leaders, we made an effort to interview a diverse sample of Fellows in the areas of race/ethnicity, career experiences, and specializations. This effort resulted in uncovering stories of crucibles related to gender and racial discrimination and cultural identity. The interviews were conducted between June 2022 and August 2023. The sample included 21 women and 19 men, 28 of the Fellows identified as White/Caucasian (70%), 6 were Black/African American (15%), 4 were Hispanic/Latino (10%), and 2 were Asian Americans (5%). In comparison, the U.S. Bureau of Labor Statistics reported that in 2022, 64% of public relations and fundraising managers were women, 87.4% were white, 8.9% African Americans, 7.5 % Hispanic/Latinos, and 2.9% Asian Americans.

It's important to trace the beginning of the PRSA College of Fellows in order to understand their mission and prestige in the industry. The Public Relations Society of America founded the College of Fellows in 1989 for the purpose of enhancing the professionalism and status of public relations (30 Years of Leadership and Legacy, 2019). In fact, this book features three inductees from the second induction class in 1990 including Ann Barkelew (see photo), who chaired the Task Force on Professionalism with Patrick Jackson, which ultimately led to the creation of the College of Fellows (30 Years of Leadership and Legacy, 2019).

The inspiration for this honorary organization came during a meeting in Chicago titled "The Itasca Symposium: The Architecture of Professional Progression"; among the industry leaders present were Edward Bernays, one of the renowned pioneers of this discipline, and Patrick Jackson, the editor of *pr reporter*, which was considered the recognized newsletter for the public relations industry from 1976–2001 (30 Years of Leadership and Legacy, 2019;

DOI: 10.4324/9781003451709-2

Figure 2.1 Chester Burger (center), the first chair of the College of Fellows, and Larry Foster (right), both members of the inaugural class, welcome Ann Barkelew into the College of Fellows during the 1990 induction ceremony.

Patrick Jackson, n.d.). The first class selected for induction into the PRSA College of Fellows was comprised of past Gold Anvil winners, PRSA's highest individual award, which is consistent with receiving a lifetime achievement award (PRSA Gold Anvil, n.d.). In fact, we interviewed seven Gold Anvil winners for this project (see Table 2.1). The first class comprised 26 public relations icons, including Edward Bernays, Pat Jackson, Harold Burson, Rex F. Harlow (one of the founders of PRSA), and just one woman, Betsy Plank. Even today, this elite group averages 350 active members, as longtime members retire or pass away and new members are inducted. Under current guidelines, PRSA members must have at least 20 years of professional experience in the discipline of public relations, achieve and maintain their accreditation (APR), make significant contributions to the discipline, and be considered role models in the profession and the community to be eligible to apply for induction (PRSA College of Fellows, n.d.). Evidence of these accomplishments is demonstrated through an application, which requires documentation of 20 case studies along with personal references that validate excellence in the areas of outstanding performance, advancement of the profession, service and leadership, and empowerment of others. J.W. Arnold, the 2023 chair of the College of Fellows, explained their high expectations:

> We talk a lot in the College about "footprint." What is that footprint you're leaving? I think that we're seeing even more emphasis on, to use the phrase of one of my predecessors, outcomes versus outputs. And when we're in

that process of evaluating an application, we're asking if he or she just did their job and did it well or was there something special? Was there something extra? What was that impact? To me that seems to be the differentiator, more so now. What is that lasting impact? There are a lot of great PR practitioners and so we're looking for those people who are truly exceptional.

Table 2.1 Life Story Interview Participants

Name	Year Inducted
J.W. Arnold, APR, Fellow PRSA	2016
Mary Deming Barber, APR, Fellow PRSA	2003
Ann H. Barkelew, Fellow PRSA	1990
Barbara A. Burfeind, APR+M, Fellow PRSA	2012
Jeremy Charles Burton, APR, Fellow PRSA	2022
Frederick H. Cook, Fellow PRSA*	2014
Ron Culp, Fellow PRSA*	2015
Anthony W. D'Angelo, APR, Fellow PRSA	2008
Kelly J. Davis, APR, Fellow PRSA	2020
Jane Dvorak, APR, Fellow PRSA	2010
Mark Dvorak, APR, Fellow PRSA	2013
Michelle Egan, APR, Fellow PRSA	2016
Geri A. Evans, APR, Fellow PRSA	2014
Gayle Lynn Falkenthal, APR, Fellow PRSA	2016
Bob Frause, APR, Fellow PRSA	1999
Amiso M. George, Ph.D., APR, Fellow PRSA	2010
Gene L. Hall, APR, Fellow PRSA	2003
Kenneth T. Hagihara, APR, Fellow PRSA	2019
Margaret Ann Hennen, APR, Fellow PRSA	2009
Dean A. Kruckeberg, Ph.D., APR, Fellow PRSA*	1990
Blake D. Lewis, III, APR, Fellow PRSA	2005
Kena L. Lewis, APR, Fellow PRSA	2022
James E. Lukaszewski, ABC, APR, Fellow PRSA	1993
Mark W. McClennan, APR, Fellow PRSA	2018
Michael L. McDougall, APR, Fellow PRSA	2015
Debra A. Miller, Ed.D., APR, Fellow PRSA *	2000
Renea Morris, APR, Fellow PRSA	2021
Mickey G. Nall, APR, Fellow PRSA *	2008
Christian "Chris" Patterson, APR, Fellow PRSA	2021
Judith T. Phair, APR, Fellow PRSA*	1994
Cheryl I. Procter-Rogers, APR, Fellow PRSA*	2000
Bey-Ling Sha, Ph.D., APR, Fellow PRSA	2022
Stacey Smith, APR, Fellow PRSA	2006
Philip Tate, APR, Fellow PRSA	2012
Ana Toro, MA, APR, Fellow PRSA	2016
Marisa Vallbona, APR, Fellow PRSA	2008
Rebecca Minjarez Villarreal, APR, Fellow PRSA	2022
Dennis L. Wilcox, Ph.D., APR, Fellow PRSA	1990
Olga Mayoral-Wilson, APR, Fellow PRSA	2014
Ira W. Yellen, APR, Fellow PRSA	2006

* Indicates Gold Anvil Winner

Since members of the PRSA College of Fellows have been officially recognized by their peers as leaders in the discipline and are required to exemplify ethical practices as defined by the PRSA Code of Ethics, many of these Fellows may be considered role models.

While the Fellows can be considered as moral exemplars, it is important to note that they are not without faults, but they still exemplify "widely shared ideas of what it means to be a highly moral person" (Colby & Damon, 1992, p. 27). Some of the criteria previously used to select moral exemplars for a similar study included:

> 1) "a sustained commitment to moral ideals or principles . . . or a sustained evidence of moral virtue," 2) "a disposition to act in accord with one's moral ideals or principles," 3) "a willingness to risk one's self-interest for the sake of one's moral values," 4) "a tendency to be inspiring to others . . . and move them to moral action," and 5) "a sense of realistic humility about one's own importance relative to the world at large."
>
> (Colby & Damon, 1992, p. 29)

Regarding humility, Colby and Damon (1992) pointed out that it "does not imply that exemplars show false modesty about their often impressive accomplishments . . . but they do not look down contemptuously at those who have accomplished less" (p. 32). Prior research has provided support that studying the life stories or narratives of exemplars matters because others may admire and desire to emulate their behaviors (Zagzebski, 2015; Van de Ven et al., 2019).

Early Leadership and Inspirational Experiences

Some of the Fellows mentioned involvement in Cub Scouts/Boy Scouts, Girl Scouts, student government, ROTC [Reserve Officers' Training Corps], and FFA [Future Farmers of America] as experiences that helped them develop leadership skills and a commitment to community service (i.e., *communion*). Gene Hall mentioned the first time he encountered the state officers in FFA, which could be considered an *originating event*:

> And they were so smooth and they were so charismatic. They tended to be the people in the community that in the towns that were leaders at various levels, at church, even athletically . . . But these guys were so remarkable that I, sitting there with my cheap cowboy hat and my boots and my FFA jacket from Newton, Texas, I said to myself, "I want to be one of those guys." And that was really the first goal of my life that I really wanted to reach. And I set about doing that. I ran for district office the next year and was secretary, which was the third ranking office. And then I ran the next

year for area and was first vice president, which was the second highest office. And I lost out to a young man who happened to have been born on the same day I was . . . I finished second and made the commitment to go and try it again the next year. And at that time, I was successful. And so, I traveled around East Texas making speeches, motivational speeches for the most part, and talking about the FFA and the opportunities that were lying there.

Who would have known that Hall would later become the spokesperson for the Texas Farm Bureau and frequently make appearances with national media organizations.

Philip Tate described an *originating event* from his childhood that prepared him for a career in sports communications. His father was working as a financial aid director at the University of Mississippi (Ole Miss) in Oxford, which placed him in the right location to pursue a rare opportunity:

I started working in the Ole Miss press box for football games when I was 13 years old. So, I was a junior high school volunteer. At my dad's urging, I went over to the athletic department offices one day after school and met with Bobo Champion, who was the assistant sports information director at the time. And I'm sure just to get rid of me, he said, "Well, here's about four banker's boxes of old baseball scorebooks. I'd like you to organize the stuff here. We've just never gotten it all pulled together." I'm sure Bobo gave me that assignment in hopes of running me off. He probably figured I would never complete that task and I would be out of his hair. Well, I finished the project in about three weeks, came back to the office and said, "What can I do next?" So, Bobo started giving me more and more stuff to do, probably because I was free labor. This was at a time when athletic departments were smaller, which meant there were great opportunities to learn, to see how to interact with coaches, work with administrators, and meet with members of the media who would come to Ole Miss for games, practices, media days and everything else. And I was learning all that as a teenager, which I found to be very helpful for working in public relations, publications, marketing, promotions and branding – all the things I've done over the course of my professional career.

This account demonstrates initiative and hard work. Following those school day experiences, Tate would later work in the athletic department throughout his college career at Vanderbilt and even managed media operations for the NCAA basketball tournament during his junior year. He then worked in sports communications during the first phase of his professional career before transitioning to agency public relations.

J.W. Arnold was fortunate to receive a scholarship from the Rotary Foundation to complete a year of graduate school in New Zealand, and one of the principles he took away from the experience is the global service organization's Four-Way Test for decision making (e.g., *memorable message*):

> And the brilliant part of the Four-Way Test is that it's so darn simple. Is it the truth? Is it fair to all concerned? Will it build goodwill and better friendships? Is it beneficial to all concerned? Four questions that hundreds of thousands of Rotarians around the world recite from memory every week at their meetings. It's profound.

Bob Frause described his involvement in the ROTC program as a young adult and a *memorable message* he took away from the experience:

> When I went to a summer camp – ROTC summer camp – I was just still a student at Fort Lewis, and the one thing that I remember more than anything else is that every day, a new officer would be in charge of the company. And so one day you were leader, and the next day you're just one of the followers down in the company, and the one thing that I remember – I don't know what the sergeant's name was – but the one thing he says was that he wanted to let everybody know that their job as a follower is to follow exactly what the leader said, and if you screw up or don't do something when it's your turn to be leader, you can count on that guy to screw it up – to make you look bad as well. So, it's essentially: leadership is learning how to follow – it's not learning how to lead, it's learning how to follow. And then, once you know how to follow, you can translate that into the feelings of people that you're trying to lead, and you understand that sometimes you have to make hard decisions, sometimes you have to be forceful, but other times, you essentially have to try to help them figure out how to get from point X to point Y, and I think that whole leadership discovery was probably one of the best things that ever happened to me: being in the Army and being a captain.

Familial and Memorable Experiences

Cheryl Procter-Rogers discussed how her parents raised her to be generous and compassionate toward others, experiences which served as *anchoring events* in her life:

> You could come home and there'd be somebody sitting at the kitchen table and it's like "who is that?" "Oh, this is so and so." "Or Cheryl, go in that closet and you got some clothes in there you're not wearing and put them in this box." What? "So and so had a fire and we're taking these clothes over." "Who is that?" "Doesn't matter who it is."

This example illustrates how impactful it can be when family members model values and virtuous behaviors instead of just preaching about their importance (Vardeman & Schauster, 2021). Experiences like these from childhood and adolescence can have a lasting impact on one's moral awareness and future behaviors (Vardeman & Schauster, 2021). Moral awareness refers to "a person's recognition that his or her potential decision or action could affect the interests, welfare, or expectations of the self or others in a fashion that may conflict with one or more ethical standards" (Butterfield et al., 2000, p. 982). This moral awareness includes the "ability to assess the moral character and vice in oneself and others" (Vardeman & Schauster, 2021, p. 213). Hursthouse (1999) explained the role of virtues and vices in moral behavior; "not only does each virtue generate a prescription – do what is honest, charitable, generous – but each vice a prohibition – do not do what is dishonest, uncharitable, mean" (p. 36). The moral instruction Procter-Rogers received was impactful because it was "frequent, consistent, and occur[ed] over a long span of time" (Vardeman & Schauster, 2021, p. 207). Who would have known that Procter-Rogers would later experience loss and the generosity of others in her own life:

> I was thinking about how many years I gave money to the Red Cross because the Red Cross came to our aid when our apartment caught on fire. And this becomes spiritual . . . It was so weird because I had my PR practice in my home. The firemen had thrown a lot of our belongings out of the apartment on the street, right? . . . And so, I'm searching through the items tossed on the street, seeing what I might salvage. All of the Kodak consultant checks were all just sitting on the ground, like, right on top. Like God said, "Girl come over here and get these checks" . . . what made this so incredible was this was a backdraft fire. So, a hot ball of fire went throughout the apartment. The refrigerator was now like a piece of sculpture. But all of the photo albums were intact. They were just singed around the edges. Certainly, the checks, mere paper would have burned. And so, the lesson there for me? I was experiencing trauma but also divine intervention. It took me less than a month to be back in business . . . Then all my family and friends, including celebrities I had worked with brought clothes, toys, and other items for our daughter. And the Red Cross gave us a voucher for clothing, food, and an apartment paid for three months. So, we were made whole pretty quickly.

Geri Evans learned about the importance of volunteer service through her parents, a legacy which she and her siblings have carried on:

> Here is in our family's DNA – my brothers and sister and our children – a desire to help others. We are here on earth for a short period of time and so the question that is critical to humankind is, "What can we do to help? How can we help?" It's special that my mom and dad were named Citizens of the Year in the Wisconsin town where I grew up as were my

brother and his wife where they live in Minnesota. My sister was recently honored for her countless hours of helping with several nonprofits in California, and I have had the honor of two named awards (from the Sunshine District and the Orlando Chapter) for distinguished service throughout my public relations career as well as special acknowledgement of my community involvement. I believe that we have an unfinished mission on this earth and part of that mission is recognizing that there is always going to be someone in need and, thankfully, there is always going to be an opportunity to help somewhere. We just need to grab hold of that opportunity.

Ann Barkelew was inspired by the actions of her mother during the Civil Rights era, including her participation in marches in Missouri. She described one moment in particular at church that taught her about courage, kindness, and inclusion:

> When the president of Lincoln University who was Black, Dr. Dawson and his wife, came to join our church once churches began to integrate, and always at the end of the service, the minister would invite the people that were going to become new members. And then the congregation would come down and greet them and welcome them to the church. Well, the day that the Dawsons joined the church, my mother, who was the choir director and the director of music in the church, came out of the choir loft and recommitted to the Methodist church with them that day and stood at the front of the church almost like saying to the rest of the congregation, "I dare you to not come down here and greet the Dawsons." And so, I always thought that that's who I want to be – the one who steps forward and says, I'm going to try to lead by example and be the kind of person that would not be afraid to stand up for what was right.

Dr. Dennis Wilcox also had a memorable experience during the Civil Rights era while reporting for his college newspaper:

> In my junior year, I decided to go on a civil rights ride down South because it's 1960 to 1961. So, I said, okay, I'm going down the South to see what's going on here in terms of that. And that was a major event in my life because it changed my whole concept of the problems that Blacks have and what was going on in terms of civil rights and stuff like that. It really came home to me . . . What was interesting was we were trying to avoid being arrested because we were meeting with students at these black universities. And so rather than go to the Woolworths and sit with them at the counter, we said, okay, we'll just go with them to the black part of the restaurant . . . So, we got arrested for going into the "colored" section and trying to eat in the "colored" section.

Dr. Wilcox said the experience led him to become more empathetic and supportive of the Civil Rights movement. Hoffman (2001) defined empathy as a "the involvement of psychological processes that make a person have feelings that are more congruent with another's situation than with his own situation" (p. 30); and Tompkins (2009) described empathy as "the experience of an Other's emotional state as one's own emotional state" (p. 65). "Empathy increases our connections to others" (Wildermuth et al., 2017, p. 19) and "dissolves the barriers between self and others. When we feel another's pain, we become connected in a shared reality" (Pavlovich & Krahnke, 2012, p. 133). Enhanced empathy may lead to a stronger desire to help others as it did for Dr. Wilcox (Wildermuth et al., 2017).

Overcoming Childhood Challenges

A few of the Fellows succeeded despite facing challenges during their childhoods. Ken Hagihara lost his father to a heart attack when he was in fifth grade and found himself struggling in school and in finding acceptance by his stepdad. He later found direction and purpose by joining the U.S. Air Force:

> I remember when I came back that first year, one of the first things my stepdad said to me was, "You've changed." I said, "Yes, sir. I learned respect. I learned the value of hard work." I realized that every time after that point, it was about proving myself. I had to prove that I was worth something. And so that's reflected in my master's degree, and reflected in my career. It's reflected in my teaching and was reflected in my desire to join the College of Fellows. I was almost a high school dropout. This campaign, I guess went a long way to prove to myself that I'm not that guy.

Kena Lewis was raised by her grandmother and two great aunts, who she said probably had a third grade education, but instilled moral values that she lives by today:

> They taught us what's right and wrong. And so, my moral compass always leans toward what I learned growing up, and I think that's kind of true for everyone . . . Some things are just wrong. You just don't – you don't lie. You don't steal. You don't treat people badly . . . if it would embarrass me in grandma's eyes to do something, oh, yeah, I'm not gonna do it.

This example proves that grandparents and extended family members can have a positive moral influence on children and adolescents. All of these experiences from their childhood and as young adults shaped the Fellows as leaders and their core values.

Notable Leader Characteristics

Similar to previous leadership research (Bennis & Thomas, 2002), a few common characteristics stood out among the Fellows. Yes, they exhibited adaptive capacity (i.e., problem solving capabilities), optimism, and neoteny (i.e., youthful qualities), which were found in previous crucible research (Bennis & Thomas, 2006), but also notable is their lifelong learning mindset, which is linked to characteristics such as curiosity, strategic thinking, and resilience (Drewery et al., 2020). Drewery et al. (2020) described curiosity as a desire to learn new things and reduce the tension tied to a lack of knowledge; strategic thinking refers to focusing on the "big picture," and being "purposeful" with specific goals and objectives; and resilience is "the capability of individuals to cope successfully in the face of change, adversity, and risk" (Stewart et al., 1997, p. 22). Lifelong learning can involve seeking both formal and informal learning opportunities (Candy et al., 1994).

Other characteristics observed that have previously been identified among Fellows were a love for learning, a concern for fairness/justice, and genuine care for others (Plaisance et al., 2023) (see Sidebar). Based on survey research with Fellows, Plaisance et al. (2023) found that they scored high for idealism (i.e., belief that the right action results in favorable outcomes) and low for relativism (i.e., rejection of universal moral rules) when evaluating ethical issues (Forsyth, 1980). The majority were classified under the Absolutist category, which means they are "confident that desired outcomes, including minimizing harmful effects, are best attained by following what they perceive to be universal moral laws addressing issues of fairness, respect and justice" (Plaisance et al., 2023, p. 7). The survey results also revealed that overall, the Fellows were moderate in political orientation (Plaisance et al., 2023).

Some other characteristics previously exhibited by exemplars included moral courage, certainty among risk, positivity, and hopefulness (Colby & Damon, 1992). In a previous study, Colby and Damon (1992) found that rather than weighing the costs and consequences of ethical behavior, exemplars tended to consider risks as "inevitable companions to living according to one's beliefs," so they are not "tormented by fear or paralyzed by indecision"

Col. Christian Patterson described his care and desire to develop others as a leader:

> I really care about people, and I really care about seeing them being able to realize their potential so that they can grow, develop, and succeed

Figure 2.2 Col. Christian Patterson serves as commander of the U.S. Army Engineer Research and Development Center, headquartered in Vicksburg, Mississippi.

and then extend that success to their families regarding opportunities and finances. So, when I was the director of communications at ERDC [U.S. Army Engineer Research and Development Center], you know, I looked at the situation there and a lot of people were telling me they're like, Chris, you've got an excellent plan but some people will have to retire for you to actually execute it. The key in those types of situations is that you can't have a defeated mindset. You have to find a way to be resilient and be able to work within those systems to achieve success for the organization and those that you lead. Hopefully when people start to see day breaks during these types of situations, they'll buy into the plan.

(p. 70). Positivity meant "setting aside bad events . . . by not focusing on them or by finding a way to construe them into a hopeful way; or it may mean finding a way to turn them to one's advantage," or accepting them as challenges to meet (Colby & Damon, 1992, p. 265). Consistent with this perspective, Dr. Amiso George said:

Like my late parents always said to me, especially my dad, you will always be challenged. Someone is going to do something to upset you every day. It is entirely up to you – how you choose to respond. That's in your power, how you choose to respond.

Jane Dvorak listed her virtue as a sense of humor, which is tied to resilience and creativity. As she explained:

> Laughter will help you through anything and everything. At your toughest times, you need it to break the tension. At the best of times, you need it to fully enjoy and pull from that energy. I think when we laugh, we learn. When we laugh, we become innovative and creative. We can find solutions because we're having fun and we're not limited. We're not limited by someone's view of how it should be done.

Personal Growth and Recognizing Vices

Another core characteristic of exemplars is continued personal growth. "They critically examine old habits and assumptions . . . adopt new strategies . . . and take up unexplored challenges" (Colby & Damon, 1992, p. 167). Consistent with these practices is awareness of personal vices or undesirable characteristics such as impatience and a tendency toward workaholism. Anthony D'Angelo described his personal struggle:

> At one point in my life, I felt like I had a white knuckle grip on that steering wheel, you know, for control and for work. I really thought at various points in my life that I could work my way through anything. Well, you know what? If I'm doing a really good job and getting a lot of kudos for 60 hours a week, well, let's turn it up a notch. You know what I mean? . . . And then all that can be rewarding for a while and then it can be debilitating. And that's the kind of struggle that I've had.

Blake Lewis described one season of his life as "extreme" and "unhealthy." He worked as both a consultant and later as an employee for the same global company. He described one example of the demands:

> I would go and I'd work in Europe for three or four weeks straight. I flew home once on a Friday to go to my daughter's high school graduation, [and] I was back at my desk in Germany, Monday morning on time. 16,000 miles total in the air, over one weekend.

As this proved unsustainable, he eventually started his own consultancy to improve his quality of work and family life (more in Chapter 4).

Other characteristics worth mentioning, much like the U.S. population in general,[1] several of our study participants have been divorced and/or

---

1 U.S. Bureau of Labor Statistics. www.bls.gov/opub/ted/2013/ted_20131108.htm

remarried; and even though most of the Fellows were raised with a Judeo-Christian background, many no longer are active members of a religious congregation, which is also consistent with national trends.[2] However, many of the Fellows discussed attending private Catholic schools or universities and attributed Jesuit teachings as the foundation of their ethical and moral values.

Questions to Consider

1. What are some examples from your childhood of times when parents, legal guardians, or educators taught you moral lessons through modeling virtuous behavior? And how has this impacted you as an adult?
2. What are some of your character strengths and weaknesses? And which of those weaknesses do you need to address and why?
3. Did you notice any characteristics of the Fellows that are consistent with your own personal strengths? If so, which ones?

References

30 Years of Leadership and Legacy. (2019). *PRSA college of fellows.* www.prsa.org/docs/default-source/about/get-involved/college-of-fellows/history-of-the-college-of-fellows-30th-anniversary-december-2019.pdf?sfvrsn=6025fa50_0

Bennis, W. G., & Thomas, R. J. (2002). *Geeks and geezers: How era, values, and defining moments shape leaders.* Harvard Business School Publishing.

Bennis, W. G., & Thomas, R. J. (2006). Crucibles. *Leadership Excellence, 23*(7), 15.

Butterfield, K. D., Treviño, L. K., & Weaver, G. R. (2000). Moral awareness in business organizations: Influences of issue-related and social context factors. *Human Relations, 53*(7), 981–1018. https://doi.org/10.1177/0018726700537004

Candy, P., Crebert, G., & O'Leary, J. (1994). *Developing lifelong learners through undergraduate education.* National Board of Employment, Education and Training.

Colby, A., & Damon, W. (1992). *Some do care: Contemporary lives of moral commitment.* MacMillan, Inc.

Dimock, M. (2019). Defining generations: Where Millennials end and generation Z begins. *Pew Research Center.* www.pewresearch.org/short-reads/2019/01/17/where-millennials-end-and-generation-z-begins/

Drewery, D. W., Sproule, R., & Pretti, T. J. (2020). Lifelong learning mindset and career success: Evidence from the field of accounting and finance. *Higher Education, Skills and Work – Based Learning, 10*(3), 567–580. https://doi.org/10.1108/HESWBL-03-2019-0041

2 NPR. www.npr.org/2021/03/30/982671783/fewer-than-half-of-u-s-adults-belong-to-a-religious-congregation-new-poll-shows

Forsyth, D. R. (1980). A taxonomy of ethical ideologies. *Journal of Personality and Social Psychology, 39*(1), 175–184. https://doi.org/10.1037/0022-3514.39.1.175

Hoffman, M. L. (2001). *Empathy and moral development: Implications for caring and justice.* Cambridge University Press.

Hursthouse, R. (1999). *On virtue ethics.* Oxford University Press.

Neuman, S. (2021). Fewer than half of U.S. adults belong to a religious congregation, new poll shows. *NPR.* www.npr.org/2021/03/30/982671783/fewerthan-half-of-u-s-adults-belong-to-a-religious-congregation-new-poll-shows

Patrick Jackson. (n.d.). https://patrickjacksonpr.com/

Pavlovich, K., & Krahnke, K. (2012). Empathy, connectedness and organisation. *Journal of Business Ethics, 105*(1), 131–137. https://doi.org/10.1007/s10551-011-0961-3.

Plaisance, P. L., Neill, M., & Chen, J. (2023). Moral Orientations and Traits of public relations exemplars. *Journal of Public Relations Research.* https://doi.org/10.1080/1062726X.2023.2250034

PRSA College of Fellows. (n.d.). www.prsa.org/home/get-involved/college-of-fellows

PRSA Gold Anvil. (n.d.). www.prsa.org/conferences-and-awards/awards/individual-awards/gold-anvil-award

Stewart, M., Reid, G., & Mangham, C. (1997). Fostering children's resilience. *Journal of Pediatric Nursing, 12*(1), 21–31.

Tompkins, P. S. (2009). Rhetorical listening and moral sensitivity. *International Journal of Listening, 23,* 60–69.

U.S. Bureau of Labor Statistics. (2013). *Marriage and divorce rates among baby boomers vary by educational attainment.* www.bls.gov/opub/ted/2013/ted_20131108.htm

U.S. Bureau of Labor Statistics. (2022). *Labor force statistics from the current population survey.* www.bls.gov/cps/cpsaat11.htm

Van de Ven, N., Archer, A. T. M., & Engelen, B. (2019). More important and surprising actions of moral exemplars trigger stronger admiration and inspiration. *The Journal of Social Psychology, 159*(4), 383–397. https://doi.org/10.1080/00224545.2018.1498317

Vardeman, C., & Schauster, E. (2021). Familial experiences of exemplars in marketing communication. *Journal of Media Ethics, 36*(4), 202–219.

Wildermuth, C., De Mello e Souza, C. A., & Kozitza, T. (2017). Circles of ethics: The impact of proximity on moral reasoning. *Journal of Business Ethics, 140,* 17–42.

Zagzebski, L. (2015). Exemplarism and admiration. In C. B. Miller, R. M. Furr, A. Knobe, & W. Fleeson (Eds.), *Character: New directions from philosophy, psychology and theology* (pp. 251–268). Oxford.

3 Development of Identity

Introduction

One of the core reasons to study crucibles is their role in developing a leader's personal identity. Identity refers to a "sense of self" and one's purpose in life (Oetzel, 2009). Crucibles lead to significant questions being considered such as: "Who am I? Who could I be? Who *should* I be?" These are times of critical reflection "when one transcends from a narrow self-regard and reflects on the self in relation to others" (Bennis & Thomas, 2002, p. 99). There are several concepts that are essential to understand when studying identity. First, *avowed identity* refers to when someone "identifies with a cultural group and asserts that membership," while *ascribed identity* is assigned to someone by others or "externally imposed" and "may not be the same as the person's avowed cultural identity" (Sha, 2006, p. 52; Hecht et al., 1993; Oetzel, 2009). In fact, one type of crucible experience can be an encounter or identity crisis, when someone is confronted with an *ascribed cultural identity*. For example, Dr. Bey-Ling Sha recounted a traumatic experience while studying abroad in France as a college student:

> The first time I ever got racially macro-aggressed was actually walking in Strasbourg. I was walking with a friend in the program, a Jewish American woman who had grown up in Chicago, and this random French dude came up to us and starts screaming in French, "Japanese, go home. France is not a Japanese colony." It was really shocking because I was a young woman. Nobody had ever been so racially aggressive to me in that way. So, I was really quite shocked and very upset and was just crying.

Dr. Sha explained that her *avowed identity* was an American, specifically a Texan which is where she was raised. Her identity also includes her Chinese cultural heritage due the fact she was born in Taiwan and immigrated to the United States at the age of 2.

Scholars have suggested that cultural identity is not always salient in children who learn about their cultural heritage from their parents and may not be

DOI: 10.4324/9781003451709-3

aware of cultural differences. According to the model of cultural identity formation (Oetzel, 2009; Phinney, 1993), individuals can experience three stages: unexamined cultural identity, identity search, and achieved identity. The first stage has been referred to as *unexamined cultural identity* (Phinney, 1993) or *pre-encounter* (Cross, 1978). The next stage of cultural identity development is referred to as *cultural identity search* (Phinney, 1993), which can be triggered by an incident or crucible experience such as the one described by Dr. Sha. Another Fellow, Marisa Vallbona, who has a Spanish cultural heritage, actually confronted these issues as a young child. As she described:

> The most vivid memory that I have of my early childhood is one when my father dropped me off at preschool and he handed me to the teacher. I was two and a half years old, and he said, "We think she understands English, but we're not sure.?" . . . And I did understand English because I have three older siblings. They spoke English at home. My parents only spoke Catalan and Spanish in the home and they told secrets to each other in French. So, our dinner table was like the United Nations, you know, our parents addressing us in their respective foreign languages and the siblings speaking to each other in English.

Vallbona initially struggled with her parents' decision to raise her to be multilingual. She described her emotions:

> I remember reading my report cards when they would be given to us by our teachers. And I remember sitting in a corner in the early grades and reading the teachers' comments, where they would say to my parents, "You're doing a disservice to Marisa by only speaking to her in Spanish at home because her vocabulary is poor, her reading skills are poor, and she needs to speak English at home." And I remember feeling a sense of shame over that, and I didn't like that feeling. And I remember being angry at my parents for that. I also remember the shame and embarrassment I felt when I'd go shopping with my mom if she'd speak to me in Spanish . . . just feeling like I hoped none of my classmates were there at the store so they wouldn't hear it. My parents would explain to me about brain development and how when you speak foreign languages, it makes you a lot smarter. My father was a M.D. and my mother a Ph.D., very, very smart parents. And so, they knew and they insisted and they said we're not changing that. And then suddenly, I would say it was about – between first, second and third grade, suddenly my vocabulary and reading skills skyrocketed, and I felt like I really shot ahead and school became so easy for me. So that was something where I learned to trust.

These emotions can be a sign of *acculturative stress*, which can be caused by issues such as perceived discrimination, English language difficulties,

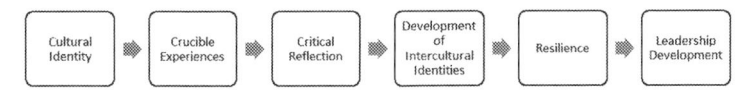

Figure 3.1 Crucible experiences model on immigrant and first-generation Latina leaders in public relations (Vasquez & Neill, 2023a).

cultural and social isolation, and bicultural stress, which is associated with maintaining separate and conflicting identities (Cruz & Blancero, 2017). To successfully cope with these stressors, individuals need to develop a bicultural identity that embraces both their ethnic and host cultures while at the same time maintaining their ethnic identity. Other successful coping strategies include developing bilingual fluency and social connections (Cruz & Blancero, 2017). Additional strategies that have been identified to cope with these stressful situations include taking action, rational thinking, seeking emotional support, identifying instrumental support (e.g., asking a friend for advice), emotional venting, avoiding the issue, positive thinking, and denial (Duhachek, 2005).

Vallbona demonstrated successful coping by working hard to develop her bilingual language fluency and now embraces her cultural heritage and childhood experiences, which included summer vacations to visit family in Spain. Vasquez and Neill (2023a) developed a theoretical model that demonstrates how cultural identity is shaped and developed through crucible experiences (Figure 3.1). The model is based on the experiences of Latina public relations leaders who identified as immigrants and first generation U.S. citizens. The cultural identity phase in this model is consistent with *unexamined cultural identity* (Phinney, 1993) or *pre-encounter* (Cross, 1978), as mentioned previously. The second phase in the model is the crucible experiences, which for people of color may include acculturation stressors such as racial discrimination or microaggressions (i.e., a comment or action that expresses a prejudiced attitude toward a member of a marginalized group; Merriam-Webster). The crucible stage leads to a *cultural identity search* (Phinney, 1993). The individual then engages in critical reflection that aids in the development of one's intercultural identity. Vasquez and Neill (2023a) also determined that resilience was an essential competency that was developed by Latina public relations practitioners after facing crucible experiences that had shaped them as leaders. Resilience refers to "the capability of individuals to cope successfully in the face of change, adversity, and risk" (Stewart et al., 1997, p. 22). Vasquez and Neill (2023a) suggested that because

> many immigrant and first-generation Latinas have learned to navigate two identities, two cultures, and two languages (oftentimes simultaneously), they can bring this dual mind-set and skill set to public relations and serve

as an empathetic leader and bridge-builder within their organizations and externally with different stakeholders.

(p. 12)

Of course, not everyone's cultural experience is the same. Unlike many immigrant or first-generation Latinas, Rebecca Villarreal never learned Spanish due to discrimination faced by her parents. As she explained:

My mom, I'm not sure what generation, she is a Mexican American here in this country, but my grandparents only spoke Spanish. So, it was interesting that throughout our lives I actually didn't see a lot of that culture as you would expect. And I think it was just the way my parents were raised. Speaking Spanish was frowned upon and they were punished for that. So, I struggled trying to be bilingual. And even to this day I have that desire and don't have the ability.

However, she later faced challenges in her professional career because others' *ascribed identity* for her involved expectations that she was bilingual due to her physical appearance and surname:

So, I started my career there, and I remember that when I started my job, my boss assumed that I was Catholic because it was a Catholic university, and I was Hispanic and that I was bilingual and spoke Spanish. I'm like, you've got two wrong so far, but I can definitely do the work. So that was fine. I got some books on Catholicism so I could get up to speed on that in case that came up in my work.

Notice that there was more than one identity ascribed to Villarreal – that she was bilingual and Catholic. This is referred to as *intersectionality* (Crenshaw, 1991), which can include other identities such as gender, race, economic and social class, and even religion. The expectation to be bilingual led Villarreal to eventually move to the suburbs, a way of avoiding the issue (Duhachek, 2005):

I didn't realize how important being bilingual was until I moved to San Antonio. So being a communicator who is not bilingual and trying to get a job and get ahead and communicate with all of your audiences is challenging if you're not bilingual. And the fact that I can't speak Spanish fluently does challenge the opportunities I have. That's probably why we moved a little north because it just wasn't an expectation as we moved out of that inner city.

Ana Toro faced a different challenge when she moved to Georgia from Puerto Rico. Because she was bilingual, she struggled with being pigeonholed or limited to only working on multicultural campaigns:

It was initially an opportunity, but I then saw it as a challenge . . . Yes, it opened doors, but it was not the only thing that I did, and I had to try to educate leaders, and colleagues, that just because I have an accent and I spoke Spanish, that didn't mean I could not support general market campaigns and efforts. So that was a little bit of a challenge. And then becoming conscious that I have a thick accent and, you know, people could think, well, "she knows less than me because she has a thick accent."

One particularly troubling form of ascribed identity are *subjugated ascriptions*, which are "identities given to others that put them in a lower or inferior position compared to one's own group" (Oetzel, 2009, p. 75). Olga Mayoral Wilson, who was raised in Puerto Rico, faced racial discrimination when she moved to Hawaii and sought a public relations position after a successful career that had involved working for a public relations agency on high profile accounts such as American Airlines, Colgate, and Del Monte. She described the interview experience:

> I went to an interview and the main PR firm principal and owner was at the conference room. She looked at me like . . . you know, sideways – not really listening to my words but placing me somewhere in the map. What I didn't know then – I was so happy-go-lucky, open and enthusiastic. And suddenly, she stopped asking and listening and she said, "Where are you from?" I answered, "Puerto Rico." I was so proud of sharing where I'm from. Then she followed by saying, "Oh, my maid is from Puerto Rico." And then she looked at me and said, "Well, I have another meeting, but so-and-so is going to continue."

Mayoral Wilson did not get the job, and it was actually her oldest sister who explained to her what had just happened – the interviewer thought of her as a maid and not as an accomplished public relations professional.

Cheryl Procter-Rogers also faced subjugated ascriptions. Despite graduating high school early and entering college at age 15, a journalism professor told her she wasn't prepared:

> And when he asked me to come to his office after class, he handed me a drop slip for the class, and a change of major slip to leave journalism. When I was about ten years old, I had written a column for a local community newspaper which gave me confidence. I was getting encouragement from my teachers and the editor that I was a good writer. This was devastating. I couldn't wrap my head around this conversation. He said he had no idea how I even got into Bradley. "You're committing academic suicide because the high school you attended didn't have the required rigor to prepare you for college." Some of that may have been true. But at the age of 17, it devastated me so that I couldn't get out of the bed for a couple of days.

Figure 3.2 Cheryl Procter-Rogers was the second African American woman to serve as national chair of PRSA. She is currently serving as the vice chair of the International Coaching Federation and serves on the editorial board of Choice magazine for professional coaching.

Procter-Rogers said her mother wanted her to continue in journalism. They appealed his decision, and once she thought about the consequences of the appeal, she chose the option to change her major:

> And I made the decision that this was a small department. And so now I'm in his crosshairs. If he doesn't get me in this class, I mean, he has a bias. He doesn't know me, right? I might be here for 10 years trying to get a degree. And I said, "I would just really rather change my major to English or something and get the heck out of here with a degree."

She later recalled how she found social and emotional support through African American students and the sisterhood of Sigma Gamma Rho Sorority of which she is a member. This support system allowed her to thrive and benefit from her college experience. She has served as president of the Bradley University Black Alumni Alliance and was recently appointed to the Board of Trustees for Bradley University.

Kena Lewis said individual perspective matters when discussing and considering *acculturative stress:*

> I am from Shelbina, Missouri, a town with a population of about 2,000. At the time I left, about 10 of us were black. Not 10 percent. Ten. So, I went to

Figure 3.3 Kena Lewis discussed her experiences attending the University of Missouri-Columbia where she received her degree in communications.

the University of Missouri, which had a student body population of somewhere around 50,000. Black students represented about five percent of the student body or about 2,000 kids. For me, coming from where I was from, that was the biggest group of black people in one area than I have ever seen in my life. The opposite was true for my new friends who were from St. Louis or Kansas City and had grown up in predominantly black communities. They felt like they were on an island. That taught me that life is all about your perspective and that even if two people are in the exact same place now, perspective is different depending on where they're coming from. I never forget that. Every now and then I hear people complaining about someone or something and they assume that everyone has that same complaint. That's when I start asking questions to try to understand their perspective. Maybe, just maybe, they're looking at the issue from only one angle. They should stop for a minute and look at it from another perspective. Perspective matters.

Oetzel (2009) discussed a *majority identity model* that is relevant to these issues. The five phases of the model are unexamined identity, acceptance, resistance, redefinition, and integration (Hardiman, 1994). The *unexamined identity* or *pre-encounter* phase (Cross, 1978) is consistent with the minority group model of cultural identity in that individuals in the majority group are unaware of cultural differences. During the second phase, *acceptance*, "majority members internalize a racist ideology either consciously or unconsciously" and "view their own group as superior" to others (Oetzel, 2009; p. 68). This may lead to racist attitudes or activities toward the minority group members. The *resistance* phase may involve shifting "from blaming minority group members for their problems" to the majority group (Oetzel, 2009; p. 68). Later phases involve recognizing one's majority group identity but appreciating other cultural identities (Oetzel, 2009). Consistent with this later stage, Margaret Ann Hennen, whose grandfather was an immigrant from Ireland, said a high point in her career was having the opportunity to student teach in Mexico City as part of her college education:

> I think the beauty of living in another culture, seeing the universalities and commonalities that exist between people is fascinating. It's so easy to find the differences. Sometimes it's harder to find the commonalities, but it's those commonalities which bind us together as humans. And that's so important. Later in my life, I chaired the board of the Minnesota Humanities Commission, which was part of the National Endowment for the Humanities. We constantly were seeking that core of humanity that pulled us together. So many of the experiences that I had as I saw the art – the Diego Rivera murals were incredible and the detail and history within them were learnings. The trips to the Zócalo, the park – the people we would just talk to in my broken Spanish and their broken English were informative. We came together and had respect for each other.

She later drew from these cultural experiences when teaching Spanish as a high school teacher prior to beginning her career in public relations.

Philip Tate, who mentioned his family's Scottish heritage in the interview, said that he doesn't like to refer to people by labels:

> I wish more people could be more welcoming and be more open to people that don't look like them. You can learn so much being around people from different backgrounds and upbringings. I hate placing labels on people. I think it's a shortcut to actually getting to know someone. It's easy to slap a label on someone – whether it's a political affiliation, oh, they're being such a Republican or they're being such a Democrat or they're being such a liberal or they're being such a conservative. What does that even mean? And that label is going to mean something different for everyone. You don't really know until you make the time to get to know someone, hopefully on a deeper level, to determine what that means to them.

It's important to remember that we share similar motivations when negotiating our personal identities. Our needs include security, inclusion, predictability, connection to others, and consistency (Oetzel, 2009). Security is a "sense of emotional safeness with others"; inclusion refers to "when others accept us for who we are" and view our identities in a positive manner; predictability has to do with a "certainty we have about our identities during interactions with others"; connection refers to the quality of our relationships with others; and consistency is tied to cultural routines (Oetzel, 2009, pp. 71, 73). One important coping strategy that is consistent with these motivations is *social connectedness*. Cruz and Blancero (2017) recommended that Latinos build and maintain relationships with mainstream society as well as their ethnic communities and families in order to achieve career success. Relationships with colleagues both within and outside of their workplace can lead to mentoring opportunities and allow for career mobility, while social connections within the Latino community can provide social support and enhance their wellbeing (Cruz & Blancero, 2017). Of course, these same recommendations may be beneficial to other cultural groups.

The final stage of the cultural identity development model is *achieved identity*, which is described as a "clear, confident sense of one's own ethnicity" (Phinney, 1993, p. 71). Also at this stage, when confronted with negative messages about their cultural identity, individuals are able to deflect and not be demoralized by them (Oetzel, 2009). For Renea Morris, being inducted into the PRSA College of Fellows was a form of personal validation:

And what it felt like to me – what it still feels like to me is when I have hit up against the issues of being a Black woman in an executive position. When I have come into situations where I may not necessarily be appreciated or understood or acknowledged or heard. I say, "Wait. I'm good at what I do and I can prove it." That's what it does for me.

Another coping strategy associated with achieved identity is *personal advocacy*, by "asserting and advocating for themselves, especially in terms of pay equity, promotions, and pigeonholing," as demonstrated in the example shared by Toro (Vasquez & Neill, 2023b, p. 16).

It is important to note that even though identity can be relatively stable once it is developed, it is also fluid and can change over time. Dr. Sha, who specializes in research focused on identity, noticed how her identity changed when she became a mother:

Becoming a mom is life changing because all of a sudden, for many women, there is a loss of identity, right? So, you used to be Bey-Ling Sha and then all of a sudden now you go places and you're Luc's mom, and there's kind of this – Well, wait. Luc's mom is great most of the time, but Bey-Ling is still here, but nobody cared about her.

Dr. Sha then reflected on her life seasons or chapters as the development and refining of her identity:

Each of these chapters is marked by the acquisition of an additional identity. And I'm literally just now thinking of it in this conversation with you. So, coming to the United States, becoming an American, moving to Texas, becoming Texan. Going to Indiana and having some of my identities reinforced, having some of my other identities be adapted out – like my Texas accent. Going to graduate school, becoming a scholar, becoming a mom. And then growing from a professorial identity into an educational leadership identity. So, again, I wouldn't say . . . that there has been just some massive, dramatic turning point for me. It's been more up to this point of my life, a story of acquiring different identities and accommodating – I don't want to say assimilating because assimilation suggests that there is one dominant thing and the other things get absorbed into that dominant thing. So, I would rather think of it as accommodating. So, who I am today is the culmination of all of those past experiences. Even today I am still all of those other identities. I just keep adding to it.

Questions to Consider

1. What can you do to be supportive and inclusive of individuals from racial, ethnic, or cultural backgrounds that differ from your own?
2. How has your personal identity developed or evolved over time?
3. What can you do to improve your social connectedness with people inside and outside of your workplace?

References

Bennis, W. G., & Thomas, R. J. (2002). *Geeks and geezers: How era, values, and defining moments shape leaders.* Harvard Business School Publishing.

Crenshaw, K. (1991). Mapping the margins: Intersectionality, identity politics, and violence against women of color. *Stanford Law Review, 43*(6), 1241–1299.

Cross, W. (1978). The Thomas and cross models of psychological nigrescence: A literature review. *Journal of Black Psychology, 4,* 1331.

Cruz, J. L., & Blancero, D. M. (2017). Latina/o professionals' career success: Bridging the corporate American divide. *Journal of Career Development, 44*(6), 485–501.

Duhachek, A. (2005). Coping: A multidimensional, hierarchical framework of responses to stressful consumption episodes. *Journal of Consumer research, 32*(1), 41–53.

Hardiman, R. (1994). White racial identity development in the United States. In E. P. Salett & D. R. Koslow (Eds.), *Race, ethnicity, and self: Identity in multicultural perspective* (pp. 117–140). National MultiCultural Institute.

Hecht, M., Collier, M. J., & Ribeau, S. (1993). *African-American communication.* Sage.

Oetzel, J. G. (2009). *Intercultural communication: A layered approach.* Vanga Books.

Phinney, J. (1993). A three-stage model of ethnic identity development. In M. Bernal & G. Knight (Eds.), *Ethnic identity: Formation and transmission among Hispanics and other minorities* (pp. 61–79). State University of New York Press.

Sha, B.-L. (2006). Cultural identity in the segmentation of publics: An emerging theory of intercultural public relations. *Journal of Public Relations Research, 18*(1), 45–65.

Stewart, M., Reid, G., & Mangham, C. (1997). Fostering children's resilience. *Journal of Pediatric Nursing, 12*(1), 21–31. https://doi.org/10.1016/S0882-59639780018-8

Vasquez, R., & Neill, M. S. (2023a). Refined by fire: Examining acculturation, resilience, and crucible experiences of U.S. Latinas in public relations, *Journal of Public Relations Research.* https://doi.org/10.1080/1062726X.2023.2222858

Vasquez, R., & Neill, M. S. (2023b). Underpaid, undervalued, undermined: Examining the cultural identities, challenges, and coping strategies of U.S. Latinas in public relations, *Public Relations Inquiry.* https://doi.org/10.1177/2046147X231200239

4 Crucible Experiences

Introduction

The Fellows experienced every crucible that can be imagined, such as facing personal illnesses or health challenges among family members, losing a job, managing major crises for organizations, pursuing growth opportunities in their careers, and starting their own consultancies. Each crucible played a formative role in the development and cementing of each Fellows' personal goals, feelings of purpose, beliefs, and values.

Confronting Mortality

Perhaps some of the most transformative experiences were confronting their own brush with mortality or that of loved ones. Accidents or health challenges resulted in life-altering crucible experiences that forged their identities and perspectives on life. Marisa Vallbona described a tragic accident that almost ended her life at age 19:

> I got hit by a car while I was running in my neighborhood at age 19. That was back in 1983 so it was a giant Cadillac, you know, one of those earlier models of Cadillacs. Giant, heavy. It hit me on my back, threw me up on the hood, slammed me back down and ended up running over my shoulder to the point where it put tire marks on my T-shirt. It all happened in front of the neighborhood pool. The lifeguard saw it and jumped off his perch. He happened to be a high school classmate, ran out, had to give me mouth-to-mouth to resuscitate me. It was just horrendous. And I actually ended up having a near-death experience.

Vallbona still experiences chronic pain from this accident, but it has shaped her perspective on life and faith, which makes it an *anchoring event* in her life story:

> I've had chronic migraines since then. It has cost me thousands upon thousands of dollars in care and healthcare. And I have to say that that has been

DOI: 10.4324/9781003451709-4

Figure 4.1 Marisa Vallbona was fortunate to survive an accident while jogging in Texas that almost ended her life at the age of 19. She was not only able to survive but thrive in her public relations career as well as enjoy an active lifestyle of running and surfing.

the worst thing that's ever happened in my life. But it's also the best thing. And it's the best thing because it convinced me there's zero to be afraid of when it comes to dying. That God's will is really true. God does everything for a reason and anything bad that's happened to me after that, I've taken it in stride because I've always known it's like, "Okay, God, I have no idea why you're doing this, but I know you're doing it for a reason, so I'm just going to make it through this. I don't like what you're doing, but I'm eager to see how you're going to play this out."

Margaret Ann Hennen said just prior to turning age 50, she was severely injured after she was hit by a Jeep Cherokee when she was walking across a street following a dinner outing. As she explained:

I never thought I wouldn't walk. I don't know why. But my pelvis was broken in two places and the ligaments in my knee were severely torn. That was really the first time I'd been in the hospital since birth. I had nothing to draw on in terms of what do you do. But I have such a wonderful support system, including one of my cousins who is a physical therapist. And she said, "What exercises are they telling you to do?" 'I'm doing this and I'm doing that? "Okay, that's fine. You do that three times a day." I immediately revised my exercise schedule from two to three times a day. I really believe that I walk today because of the physical therapists and the physical therapy direction that I got . . . The experience was just a bit of and a rude awakening to the vulnerability of one's body and how one's body betrays you at certain points in your life. There's nothing you can do about it to prevent it. Things are just going to happen. I learned from that how important friends and community were.

Later in life, Hennen would battle lung cancer followed by a brain tumor, which was stage IV lung cancer that had migrated to her brain. What she most treasured was the quality time she spent with her mother following her surgery for lung cancer:

I'm always looking for that silver lining. And in this case, my mother came and stayed with me. My father had died about four years before that. My mom came and lived with me for two or three months. One of the things she said to me was, you know, we haven't spent this much time together since you were in high school. She was so right. I got better. She was able to be present when I was presented with an award for volunteer of the year for the St. Paul Chamber. For her to be there was really exciting for me. She went back home and about six weeks later, she died suddenly of a heart attack. That's the silver lining. Not that she died of course, but that we spent that time together.

Hennen demonstrated resilience as she coped with these health challenges by downplaying negative feelings while foregrounding positive emotions (Buzzanell, 2010). Her health scans have been negative for cancer the past two years. Gene Hall and Jeremy Burton both had to deal with health challenges involving their sons. Hall's son Chad was diagnosed with kidney cancer at age 5. As he explained:

It was called Wilms' tumor, and it's rare. He underwent surgery to remove a kidney and had 18 weeks of chemotherapy and all of the angst that goes with that. It's difficult to explain, but I kind of dreaded him going off chemotherapy because even though he was very much looking forward to it, it became a crutch. You know as long as he's on chemotherapy, he's going to live. But he did go off. We've seen no sign of the cancer since 1992.

Hall said this experience made him more family-oriented and led to his love of baseball since Chad was unable to play football.

Jeremy Burton's son battled chronic kidney issues from birth. At age 12, he required a kidney donor, and fortunately, Jeremy was a match. He described the moment he connected with his wife and son via technology prior to their surgeries:

It's a very vivid memory to pray for my son and tell him I love him before each of our surgeries even though we were in two different hospitals. There were lots of tears on both ends of the video call. I get credit for being the hero of the story because I donated my kidney, but it was my wife who was the real hero. Taking care of our son for days and she couldn't even come and see me after my surgery for almost two days. So, she was worried about two people at once. But her priority had to be for our son.

He and his wife relied on their faith to get through those difficult times. They found reassurance in a specific passage in the Bible, a *memorable message*:

And the question is why? Was it my sin or something I did that caused his sickness? My wife had the same thoughts. We found comfort in the Bible. In John 9 verses 1–4, it says,

As he passed by he saw a man blind from birth. And his disciples asked him, "Rabbi, who sinned, this man or his parents, that he was born blind?" Jesus answered, "It was not that this man sinned, or his parents, but that the works of God might be displayed in him. We must work the works of him who sent me while it is day; night is coming, when no one can work. As long as I am in the world, I am the light of the world."

We really latched on to that scripture and found comfort that God could use our situation to bring hope to others.

Mark McClennan and his wife also dealt with health issues involving their son:

When my youngest son was born, my world completely changed. We knew when my wife was pregnant, there was something that was the matter with the pregnancy. We had a test, and the doctor told us 80% chance of brain damage, 40% chance of mortality in the first year. We said, "You know what? God gave him to us for a reason." Today he's 15 and doing awesome. He has a very rare genetic syndrome. And by very rare, I mean 300 cases in the world rare. There's no real bell curve because there's not enough cases, but he's doing awesome. More people know him than know me.

McClennan discussed just how difficult those early days were for him and his family:

The first year and a half was brutal. He had "failure to thrive." We would spend one hour every three hours just to get him to drink one ounce of liquid. I was sleep deprived for two years. My wife and I would just trade off, but I was falling asleep at stoplights. But today it has given me the greatest joy. When you see this kid . . . just his attitude and the joy that he brings to everything . . . it just shows you that you can't let things limit you.

Philip Tate faced his own health challenge following an accident while working at a fast food restaurant in Mississippi just before he was planning to start college:

So, I was working there along with a couple of my dear friends. One night, my job was to dispose of the French fry grease, which meant going to dump it out back in a special container. It had rained a little bit that evening, and I slipped and fell, dumping a whole container of French fry grease on my arm. And it was awful. I suffered second- and third-degree grease burns on my arm. I had to be taken to the burn unit at Baptist Hospital in Memphis, which was about an hour away, for treatment because they couldn't treat me at the Oxford hospital in town. I was in the hospital for six to eight weeks and had multiple skin graft surgeries. The accident and recovery delayed my entrance into Vanderbilt, and I couldn't start college until January. I had to go through extensive rehab to get strength back in my arm. Obviously, that accident became a formative event in my life.

Tate said he required five to six surgeries to repair the damage to his skin. The recovery experience taught him resiliency:

> What I had to deal with following the grease burn, it delayed the start of my college career. I was jumping in, literally in the middle of the school year, as a freshman needing to meet people and make friends who had already formed most of their friendships and relationships during that fall semester. In hindsight, it probably demonstrated to me that with proper focus, dedication and consistency, you can overcome just about anything. Accidents like my grease burn are nothing you could plan. Sometimes you just have to respond to and make the best of a bad situation.

Career Setbacks

Common crucible experiences faced by the Fellows were career setbacks, such as losing a job or receiving critical feedback. Ana Toro, Jim Lukaszewski, and Mickey Nall, all faced the disappointment of a job loss twice in their careers. Toro explained how she was devastated:

> I lost my job at 50, and I was just – I couldn't believe it. I'm APR, Fellow PRSA. I had won awards. I serve on the PRSA national board. I had served in Puerto Rico. I mentor students, and I could not believe that my previous job – well, I never knew the reason, but apparently funds ended, right. That's how contractors work. You get money from the federal government and you have accounts. And with them, I was very happy for eight years. So, it was my turn, I guess. And well, it also took me eight months. The same eight months that it took me when I moved to Georgia to find a job. But this time around, I felt a sense of failure in a way, because you always hear it from other people, oh, they lost a job. Poor thing . . . but it's not the same until you go through it.

Eventually, Toro sought help from a career counselor and landed her current job with the Centers for Disease Control, which she considers to be a high point in her career.

Lukaszewski was about to lose his job for a second time in his career when a business that had acquired his firm eventually decided to part ways. It was at that very moment, he received a phone call from a public relations legend, Chester Burger. Lukaszewski had developed an indirect relationship with Burger who was a fan of his public relations columns and would send him notes from time to time:

> Chet calls, "What are you doing?" And I said, "Well, I'm at home, Chet. Not that much to do." He said, "What are you doing tomorrow?" I said, "Chet, I'm going to be out of a job in 45 minutes. I have no idea." He says, "Why don't you come to New York and work for me?" So, I looked down the hall. Barbara's [his wife] on the extension phone down there, so I asked her, "You want to go to New York?" It was thumbs up. Nine days later, this kid (Jim) from Robbinsdale [Minnesota] is walking down Madison Avenue in Manhattan, looking for #133, which is where my office and Barbara's were to be for the next three years.

Nall was laid off after a long and successful career as an agency executive at Ogilvy & Mather. This disappointment came after he had served as the national chair of PRSA:

> And it was the first time in the low point that I wasn't sure I was going to stay in our industry or business. So that's what made it low for me. It was like, What the hell? You know, gosh, I've been chair of this national, international organization. I speak all over the country. I've spoken in foreign countries. I have this big, you know, international agency I work for and I love. How's that going to compete? You know, what's next? Will it feel like such a letdown?

It was at that point that Nall accepted a professor of practice position at his alma mater, the University of Florida.

Other Fellows also faced low points in their careers. Amiso George had to deal with self-doubts when she received negative feedback from colleagues about her job performance. She reached out to family and friends for support:

> I knew deep down that what I was doing was good. My work was good. When you get that from the people who are making the decision whether you get promoted, it hurts, and then calls into question, what have I been doing? Am I wasting my time doing this? What can I learn from the critique?

She later received external affirmation when she was awarded the Outstanding Educator Award by PRSA in 2017. She later was promoted to full professor in 2020.

Similarly, Dr. Dean Kruckeberg described a low point in his career when he experienced criticism of his scholarship. He said, "But as far as a real low point, I suppose there's . . . where scholarship is rejected or something doesn't quite work out right." He cited the support of professional and academic communities in helping him have the courage to persevere. Dr. Kruckeberg explained, "That is where much of the idea of professional community becomes very important, you know, we can be good . . . even though we have these little points or criticisms, maybe together we're going to keep on."

All of these examples demonstrate the importance of not becoming demoralized by setbacks, but focusing on discovering the next opportunities.

Crises as Crucibles

Another common crucible experience for public relations leaders is managing crises. For Jeremy Burton, it was managing a crisis involving the president of Oral Roberts University, and for Blake Lewis, it was counseling the fertilizer industry which was facing lawsuits following the Oklahoma City bombing and managing a crisis following the death of a high-profile patient at a hospital where he was working. Gayle Falkenthal managed multiple crises in her career, including wildfires in San Diego and the Heaven's Gate mass suicide in 1997. Ann Barkelew counseled a children's theatre dealing with sexual abuse allegations, and Ron Culp had to manage a crisis involving negative side effects associated with a prescription drug. Kena Lewis managed the hospital's communication response following the Pulse nightclub shooting in Orlando. Barbara Burfeind was working in the Pentagon when it was struck by a plane as part of the terrorist attacks on September 11, 2001. What all of these experiences had in common were they challenged Fellows' professional skills and abilities, but also were physically, mentally and emotionally draining. Burton described his experience:

> Three or four weeks after the press announcement with allegations against the university's president, we were working 16 to 18 hour days. That type of crisis moment typically lasts a couple of weeks. This one went on for around four months. Every morning I woke up to a new major press issue. I remained the spokesperson for the university from that point until I left in 2015. Even in that adversity, I forged a good relationship with the journalists in the area through many uncomfortable interactions. Whenever I left the university, I remember a leader at the regional newspaper telling me that she felt like I raised the bar for ethics and public relations in the region. I thank God for that opportunity to be a Christian example in that way and I was proud of my work.

For Blake Lewis, a thorn in his side was the crisis he missed while visiting family for Thanksgiving. This happened in the years prior to technology innovations that now keep public relations practitioners connected. As he explained:

> And while I was on vacation, we had a VIP patient die in our facility, and I wasn't there. There were seven hospitals in the region, at a time when competition among providers was in its earliest phase and a colleague at a cross-town facility got called in by my boss . . . it was absolutely the right thing to do under the circumstances. And I was devastated.

Lewis was later presented with a *gift*, a permanent reminder of the time he wasn't there to assist with a crisis:

> But when I left the organization – let's see, it would have been three or four years later – at my going away party, one of the presents was a desk sign and on one side was my name, and on the other side was my counterpart's name from the other hospital. So, for a caring organization that was worried about the health of people, that was probably not the healthiest thing, but it was a teachable moment.

Gayle Falkenthal won a career award from the San Diego Chapter of PRSA for her crisis communication response to the Heaven's Gate mass suicide. She was working in a different department for the county at the time:

> Our county's medical examiner didn't have their own public affairs representative, and the county itself did not have a very large team. And ironically, they had a brand new chief public affairs officer. He'd been in place 10 days. And he was my old radio station boss, and it was his first PR job. So, he called my boss and said, "I need some help. Can you loan her to me?" And then quickly, the county asked my elected official boss, who was independent, "Can you loan her to the medical examiner for the next week or ten days or however long it takes, because somebody needs to run this response?"

Falkenthal said the initial media response to the incident was overwhelming:

> What it really astonished us, this took place in the late afternoon, the initial notice. By the next morning, we probably had five or six dozen international media, complete with satellite trucks, etc. there. But we kept thinking to ourselves, how did they get here so fast? The prior night had been the Academy Awards in Los Angeles, and they were all still there. And they drove down the freeway two hours. They were packing up and every one of their home country officials said, head south.

For Falkenthal, this was a high point in her career because it challenged her in so many ways:

> I kept thinking, how did I get a career PR award? I'm 38 years old. I'm gonna work a lot more. I think this might be a little premature. But I was

very proud of that moment and no, I mean, I can't say I'm happy because it came at the death of dozens of people, and it was grueling. It was a grueling assignment to deal with. And it was made easier because I was dealing with some incredibly professional people who understood what had to be done.

Ann Barkelew (see Sidebar) was a volunteer and member of the board for the Children's Theatre in Minneapolis when she provided counsel during a crisis:

And so, I think that the wisdom I had acquired doing public relations in education and for a couple of years at that point in time at Dayton Hudson, helped guide how we dealt with the crisis. None of the arts organizations had a policy how do you deal with things like sexual abuse, you know, or whatever, those kinds of things. So, because of the children's theatre crisis, we were able to pull together the arts community and each one, the orchestra, the Guthrie Theatre, the St. Paul Chamber Orchestra, the Minneapolis Institute of Arts, the Walker Art Institute – all appointed representatives and we created model codes of ethics and board responsibilities – no arts organization had those kinds of things. And so, we sort of helped create them together . . . We put all of our funding on hold. We went around and met with major funders and said, "We're not here to ask for money – we just want you to give us some time to get things organized. And when we can tell you everything is squeaky clean, we'll be back for money."

She took on this monumental task to ensure the theatre would be around for children and their families for years to come and was proud to see the theatre later receive an Emmy.

Ann Barkelew had a remarkable career in education and corporate public relations and actually was the first female executive at Dayton Hudson, now known as Target Corporation, which makes her one of the pioneers in the industry:

And I think when I was named to the management committee at Dayton Hudson, the other division heads in the corporate headquarters, I remember one of them saying, "Ann is the only one here that earned her way on." And, you know, the others, the general counsel, the chief financial officer, all of them had come into positions that were already part of the management committee. So, I think that was probably the turning point for me. And I think at that point, after I'd been doing that for a year or so and handled a crisis or two, I always felt like I could do anything, you know, if I could do that.

The next crisis scenario began on a high note. Ron Culp was working for a pharmaceutical company as it was about to launch an important new treatment for arthritis. Despite a few reports of easy-to-control side effects, the medical team assured company leaders and the PR team that the drug was safe and ready for market:

> At a management meeting the day before the launch and after only recently becoming aware of the UK reports, the company CEO asked the head of medical, "Is there any reason why Ron shouldn't launch this campaign tomorrow?" And he responded, "Absolutely not. This drug is safe and effective when used as directed" . . . So, we went to New York where we had rented the ballroom of the Waldorf Astoria hotel due to media interest in this breakthrough drug. Every major media organization was there, the big three networks, New York Times, Newsweek, Businessweek, Time – it was an amazingly impressive media turnout. We introduced them to several arthritis patients who shared their dramatic success in clinical trials . . . When I got on the corporate plane that night to fly back from New York, the company CEO happened to be on that plane although he hadn't attended the press conference. Also onboard was the head of sales, who quipped: "So I understand we can send our salesforce home tomorrow because this was such a successful event." And I said, "I just hope it wasn't too successful." A couple hours later, I get home, turned on ABC Evening News, and the lead story called it a "miracle drug" – a term we never used although patients now able to walk and return to work felt it was just that and had shared their personal stories with reporters. Electronic media stories were soon followed by major articles and cover stories in Time, Newsweek and others. Sales absolutely skyrocketed for this drug, plants were working 24/7 to produce the product and plans were made for building larger facilities in the U.S. and abroad. Analyst sales projects suggested it would be a billion-dollar drug by year end.

A few weeks after the launch, the company started receiving some reports of side effects, which required updates to prescribing information and marketing materials. As Culp explained:

> One of the side effects was photosensitivity. You go out in the sun without sunscreen, it's going to make you sick. And one of the unusual side effects is that some individual's fingernails would turn black and eventually fall off. It was early summer, so that might be expected. The medical team suggested increasing emphasis in the package literature about that possibility. But soon, more serious things happened to some other patients, especially the elderly and those with impaired renal function. In some cases, the side effects would stop when you discontinue taking the drug, but in other cases patients got very sick or even died.

Eventually, the pressure got to Culp and he lost his composure:

> After a series of FDA and Congressional hearings and a threat by the Secretary of Health & Human Services to ban the drug, the company decided to voluntarily withdraw the drug from the market. On that day, the PR team fielded nearly 400 media calls from around the world. Occasionally, a patient would reach us – either desperately seeking more of the drug before it was removed from market or to explain their personal side effects. We were physically and mentally drained. At my low point, one of my team members, John Purcell, ran into my now crowded office saying he was on a call with a woman who demanded to talk with someone regarding her fingernails that were falling off. I just looked up and said, "Tell her she's lucky to be alive." While at the time I thought my response was hysterical, others were shocked until I made it clear that I was just kidding. At that point, I realized we needed to slow down and get some rest. Today, every one of the people in the office that night will tell me that story and how they thought at the moment I'd lost my mind, but afterwards they were crying with laughter, because, they said, "That made you so real, that you were this automaton up until then. How does he remain so calm and cool?" And then that was my breaking point.

Of course, Culp did not actually say that to the woman on the phone. He added:

> I even came up with the right thing to tell her and properly commiserated, but I thought it was kind of a cruel initial thought, even if it seemed very funny at the time. So as someone who frequently uses humor in his management of others, those are the kind of things I have to be careful about.

Stung by being the first pharmaceutical product launched through PR in the United States, the company retrenched and Culp was asked to focus his team's PR efforts on internal communication going forward. His mentor and then PR consultant to the company, Jack Raymond, advised him at the time, "To really make your career take off, you've got to move to a larger market; you gotta get out of here." Shortly after that conversation, Culp accepted the director of PR position at Pitney Bowes, where he worked for two years until he was recruited to Chicago by Sara Lee Corporation. Culp's willingness to relocate to Connecticut and then Illinois demonstrates his adaptive capacity and risk taking, which eventually resulted in "new insights, new skills, new qualities of mind or character that make it possible to function on a new, higher level" (Bennis & Thomas, 2002, p. 105).

Kena Lewis also had to manage a major crisis. She received a phone call at 3 a.m. following the Pulse shooting, notifying her that there had been an incident at the nightclub in Orlando and that they were activating incident command:

> We took in about 49 patients, in various conditions, from Pulse. The first nine were so severely injured they were not survivable. We had about 30 victims who were in the hospital long term. I was so glad to have completed the Incident Command crisis training. I cannot express how important it is for people in our industry to do that. It's not enough to have a crisis plan that you never use sitting on the shelf. You have to actually practice it. On a personal note, if you've never lived in a city that experienced a tragedy of this type, a massacre, the first thing you think is 'how could someone do this in my city?' You get angry. You know, this is my town. How dare you come into my town and do this? It was just devastating. But there were also moments of triumph in all that chaos. I remember we had one patient who came to us the night it happened, June 12. And he was with us in the hospital until September. That is a long time for someone to be in the hospital. But he was able to walk out on his own power. So that whole experience, which could arguably be the lowest point in my career, also had some really heartwarming moments.

Barbara Burfeind described the horrific experience of working in the Pentagon on September 11, 2001:

> We were on the side that the plane hit, but we were in the inner rings. The Pentagon has ABCDE rings, with D and E on the outside. We were in a B ring office closer to the center . . . When the plane crashed into the building, it went all the way up to the C ring. We were between the third and fourth corridors, and it entered from the fourth, and then went over and down into the fifth corridor on the C ring. The plane stopped at the C ring. If you looked at the rings in the Pentagon, they have space between them. If you look out the window of the interior offices, you can see the other corridor. We returned two weeks later to get our stuff, because everybody evacuated, and then because of the smoke damage and mold, we couldn't return. They had to redo the offices. We had to wear Hazmat suits because of the mold and the smoke. I asked the guy who was escorting us . . . "So, did all the people get out on that C ring?" And he replied, "not everybody." Nothing really hit home until a couple of days later when I saw the list of missing, and I knew five of the people listed. And I thought, oh, my gosh, this was way too close.

Burfeind said the experience just increased their resolve:

> At that point, I had been thinking about retiring, and everybody, me and everybody else included our thoughts of leaving went out the window. It

was like, no, you're going to be here and help do whatever we can to move forward.

As difficult of these crises were to endure, the Fellows developed resilience and pushed themselves to accomplish more than they ever could have imagined. At times, it also led to mental and physical exhaustion, which will be discussed more in Chapter 5.

New Territory Crucibles

While many of these crucibles would be considered reversals or setbacks, other experiences described by the Fellows could be categorized as new territory or opportunities (Thomas, 2009). Judy Phair described the challenge of assuming the role of vice president of public relations at Goucher College at a time when women were not as prevalent in senior leadership roles. Dr. Debra Miller became the first African American woman to be chair of PRSA. Fred Cook became the unlikely CEO of Golin in Chicago. Kelly Davis successfully advocated for a tax increase on cigarettes in South Carolina to prevent smoking among youth.

Phair described how her promotion came to be:

I was director of public relations, reporting to the vice president for advancement. He left for a position at another university. We had a very good relationship. I didn't know that he recommended to the president that

Figure 4.2 Judy Phair became a vice president of public relations at a university during a time when not many women held senior leadership roles.

she make me interim vice president. She called me into her office and said, "Harry thinks you should be interim VP – what do you think?" I said, "Yes, of course." She responded, "I think so too. Let's do it." So, suddenly I was vice president over public relations and development.

Phair assumed the role in a challenging time as the college was beginning to consider potentially transitioning from a women's college to co-ed. She provided counsel on how to manage student and donor relations during that difficult season. Phair explained what made this moment a high point in her career:

This promotion was certainly in my range and ambition, but the timing was unexpected and therefore especially exciting. It tapped into what I saw as part of my future, where I wanted to go. I knew what the college was entering. I knew that it was about to seriously consider coeducation. I knew the skills that I was going to be asked to bring forward in a way that I had wanted to and didn't have much chance to do previously. I thought, wow, this is what I want. And it's going to be difficult. It's going to be challenging. But I love doing that. I love facing challenges. And I loved the opportunity to move with a leader for whom I had great respect and who respected me. A year later, Simmons hired a VP for development – and created the new and equal status position of VP for public relations, which I held for several years before moving on.

Dr. Debra Miller's journey to national chair of PRSA began with her involvement on the Minority Affairs Committee:

As a result of my work in developing communications for diverse audiences with the 1990 Census, it became clear to me that the public relations profession and PRSA was missing out on invaluable information. It was at that point that I realized that my fellow practitioners and educators did not know how to communicate with diverse audiences. The "browning" of America was beginning. My research at the time was designed to help the industry embrace these new audiences and share ways to effectively communicate with them by using strategies, tactics and channels that helped influence their behavior. This presented great opportunity and challenges for our profession. Those practitioners who became adept at communicating with these audiences (African Americans, Hispanics, Asians and Pacific Islanders) could be indispensable to their organizations. Organizations who did not embrace this new concept and the reality of our nation would be left behind. Their business and social responsibility strategy would be impacted. My research and course development served as a wakeup call for our profession.

Figure 4.3 Dr. Debra Miller was the first woman of color to become national chair of PRSA.

Dr. Miller described the effort behind her historic election as national chair of PRSA in 1997 as the first woman of color to lead the organization:

> And I always said I was going to write an article about it, what it means to be the first, because I felt that, of course, it was not something I'd done. I did not get there alone. With the help of the Minority Affairs Committee and several enlightened leaders in PRSA, we successfully implemented a strategic communications and marketing campaign. I had already served on the Board and served as Secretary. It began with nominating me from the floor for the office of Treasurer, which to my knowledge had not been done before in PRSA. After holding this office, the following year I became President-Elect. It pays to read the by-laws. [Smile] The assembly was not prepared for this. From the nominators to my speech from the floor, all of it was planned and implemented with energy, passion and commitment. We realized that this was a turning point for the profession; I realized that I was making history. It was imperative that I was not only leading PRSA, but I was making a bold statement to the industry that multicultural leaders and practitioners exist, we have a voice and we're here to stay, and more of us will be joining you in the boardrooms, classrooms and podiums across the nation and the world.

She added this moment was a dream fulfilled:

> On a personal note, no one knew that I had visualized myself in this role after I attended my first PRSA conference in New Orleans, and I was one of five people of color out of 300 other than the wait staff at the assembly. I saw myself at the podium and I promised myself that I would lead PRSA one day. Dreams do come true.

Fred Cook's career path can best be described as unconventional. He didn't begin his first job in public relations until age 36. He had spent time traveling the world, including time working on ships, serving as a tour guide, or as a doorman at a hotel. Eventually, he was working for a small firm in Los Angeles that was acquired by Golin Harris. Due to his success in L.A., Cook was transferred to the Chicago office to become president. It was a difficult transition due to a different corporate culture and a lack of personal relationships with his new colleagues:

> My first year here was really hard – no one in the Chicago office really wanted to work with me, no one knew who I was, even though I'd been in the company for a long time, and I was really having a challenging time figuring out my role and what my value was going to be. I had gone from running a very successful operation, where everybody admired me and thought I was smart and important – to sitting in the agency's headquarters, where I was simply being ignored. I wondered if moving my family to Chicago was a terrible decision.

Cook's career changed in an instant after receiving a phone call while on a family vacation:

> A year later, our parent company, Interpublic initiated a restructuring and the PR group got a new leader – Harris Diamond. I'd never met Harris, but I was aware of his "take-no-prisoners" reputation. His first call to me was when I was in London on vacation with my family – when he said, "Fred, I want you to come back to Chicago." I explained "I'll be back in a week." He firmly replied, "I want you to come back tomorrow." I asked "Why?" And he said, "I can't tell you, but you need to be here." I wasn't sure really what was up, but I left my family, and flew back to Chicago. The next day Harris came into our office for the first time and asked my boss to retire. After that short conversation, he invited me downstairs to an empty restaurant, where over a brief cup of coffee, he unceremoniously stated, "You're the new CEO."

Cook described his surprise at the new appointment and the challenges he faced:

> I was slightly shocked. I knew something was up, but I never anticipated this would happen. But as the reality sank in, I became excited about the

opportunity. I had lots of ideas of things I wanted to do and now I could actually do them. The company was really in terrible shape. We weren't winning new business, we were losing money, we'd made a lot of bad acquisitions and staff morale was really low. It was a horrible time in our history and my new job was to turn all of that around.

He later described his joy when Golin started winning awards again including Agency of the Year:

I was running in Central Park the next morning, after we had received the award, listening to the Queen song, "We are the Champions." Singing along loudly, I ran up to the top of a huge rock and thrust my arms triumphantly up in the air – hoping no one was watching! I was happy and grateful that I'd been able to lead us back to a place where we could be successful, respected and proud.

Kelly Davis worked for the Campaign for Tobacco-Free Kids to seek passage of a bill in South Carolina that would increase the cigarette tax. It was a five-year effort, but ultimately, their efforts were successful.

My proudest accomplishment professionally was when we secured an increase in our state cigarette tax with the funding going to youth smoking prevention. The cigarette tax had not been increased in almost 30 years. At that point in time, it was the lowest in the nation. And there was a lot of data that showed that for every 10% increase in the price of a pack of cigarettes, there would be a corresponding 7% decline in youth smoking rates and a 3% decline in adult smoking rates. So, the focus of our coalition was really very heavily on youth to keep a kid from ever starting to smoke. Then you prevent a lifetime of disease and the associated health care costs.

As Davis explained, the effort required perseverance and determination:

We secured a lot of bipartisan support for the legislation. We had several stops and starts – bills that started going somewhere and then got killed. And we had one bill that went all the way through the legislature, and then the governor vetoed it . . . We did eventually have to overcome a gubernatorial veto to get the bill to pass and successfully did that. And so, I think about joy – just thinking about that moment sitting in the Senate chamber, you know, two days after the House had overridden the governor's veto-sitting in the Senate chamber with our whole team and this team of people who had really become like a family because most of us have been working on this issue together five years. Some of them had been working on it for ten years. It was a very impromptu celebration. I tend to be a very emotional person, but not usually in a media interview. As a spokesperson for the coalition, my voice broke, because this has been all about the health of kids in our state. And so that moment of having worked so hard with so many people for so many years to do this was such a high point of celebration.

Starting Their Own Businesses and Suspension Crucibles

Several of the Fellows eventually started their own consultancies. Cheryl Procter-Rogers is now distinguishing herself in the realm of executive coaching:

> So about 20 years ago, I started getting more requests for executive coaching as part of my public relations and business strategy consulting. Current or potential clients would ask for a meeting to talk about my services. "I'd love to meet with you and talk to you about us perhaps working together." So, I would do all my research in preparation for getting public relations business. Once at the meeting, I often heard, "Oh no, Cheryl, I just want you to work with me as an executive or I just want you to work with my executive team as a thought partner," or something similar. I quickly learned that executive coaching was emerging as a true profession. To be better prepared for the conversations, I took some training with my fingers crossed that I was indeed coaching and not counseling. I was so happy that roughly 80% of what I was calling coaching was indeed coaching. I learned that I was coaching all of my career. How can you implement any public relations strategy without coaching the leaders?

Blake Lewis started his consultancy after realizing that he needed to prioritize his family, a *suspension* moment:

> I defined my life as either you work for the organization directly, or you work as a consultant to an organization. And I plowed all of my effort in, and I realized that was where I had tried both sides of the model that is so well known to anybody in strategic communications – you're either a consultant or you're an employee. And I had great experiences in both, but I saw deadly challenges to both in terms of quality of life and my responsibilities as a citizen of the city, county, state, federal, world environment, and most importantly, family. And so that was why I went and started my own firm, because I started with a blank piece of paper – What are the rules here, what's important, how we do things? And while the initial rules and the value sets and all that are well ensconced in 2022 at Three Box and have made it through now a second generation with lots and lots of people that have been touched. They're very much at the core, but over the 23 years, we've developed, perfected, sanded and refinished the firm. To me, that was that was a high point in my career, letting me say, "Okay, I've done all the things, I've had a career that a lot of people are shocked at,

and I just fell into much of it. Now, I have a chance to take all my learnings and design something from the ground up," and that's been an awesome experience.

Another suspension crucible occurred in Marisa Vallbona's life when her mother had a heart attack. Unfortunately, she had a demanding client at the time:

And I told the verbally abusive client that I was out of pocket for the next couple of days because of my mother. And the verbally abusive client said, "I don't care. I don't care what's going on with your family. You will be on these conference calls." And I told the client, I said, "I don't have reception in the ICU. The hospital doesn't get cell reception." You know how some areas of hospitals sometimes are blocked out. She said, "Then you go somewhere where you do get reception and you be on those conference calls." And I said, "My mom might not make it and I don't want to not be there if she passes away."

During these difficult times, Vallbona realized she longer valued awards in comparison to her family:

I looked around my mom's home office, and I saw these plaques on her wall and all these awards for the work that she had done . . . And as I looked around her office, I thought, what point is it? What is the point of all these awards of being so driven, of publishing as many novels and books as she has, of everything that she's done? When you don't spend the time with your family that you should, when you don't enjoy your life and have outside hobbies, when you don't . . . I mean, look at this beauty. Look at everything that's out there. There's just a lot more to life. And I thought, forget it. I resigned the client. I didn't care about the money. That made no difference to me. And my mom did survive the heart attack. But when I got home, I took most of my awards and I threw them in the dumpster.

She then gave her adult sons the following advice:

I told my kids. I said,

Life is not about winning awards. It's not about the work you do. The work you do is great because it says that, you know, man should produce. Man and woman should produce. God gave us a talent and we should use our talent. Yes, that's important.

I said, "But that's not what life is about. Life is about loving others. And if you're going to waste life with your nose in your work and strive to win awards, then you've wasted your potential as a human being."

As reflected in this statement, crucibles are "both an opportunity and a test," a "defining moment that unleashes abilities, forces crucial choices, and sharpens focus," and teach a "person who he or she is" (Bennis & Thomas, 2002, p. 16). In Chapter 5, the Fellows will reflect on what they have learned over a lifetime of facing multiple crucible experiences.

Questions to Consider

1. What are some defining crucibles that you have faced in your lifetime and how have these experiences shaped your priorities and values?
2. How would you categorize the crucibles you have faced (i.e., new territory, reversal, or suspension) and which ones have been the most impactful for you?

References

Bennis, W. G., & Thomas, R. J. (2002). *Geeks and geezers: How era, values, and defining moments shape leaders.* Harvard Business School Publishing.

Buzzanell, P. M. (2010). Resilience: Talking, resisting and imagining new normalcies into being. *Journal of Communication, 60,* 1–14.

Thomas, R. J. (2009). The leadership lessons of crucible experiences. *Journal of Business Strategy, 30*(1), 21–26.

5 Critical Reflection

Introduction

As the Fellows reflected on crucible experiences in their lives, they began to draw lessons from their experiences. Similar to prior research, they reflected on how these experiences shaped who they are today, what matters to them, and their values, and refined their judgment as leaders (Chance, 2021). As previously mentioned, sometimes the Fellows had to confront times when they didn't live up to their personal ideals (Byrne et al., 2018). Steele (1988) explained that we deal with these personal deficiencies by engaging in self-affirmation through explanations, rationalizations, or behaviors to maintain our self-image of a person who is "morally adequate . . . competent, good" (p. 262). Some self-affirmation approaches can include crediting successes to the self but failures to circumstances outside of their control; or engaging in activities such as prayer and conversations with friends, which may not directly address the issues but are means of coping with the stresses (Duhachek, 2005; Steele, 1988). In addition, awareness of one's personal negative traits may actually be viewed as a way of controlling them, which may outweigh their threats to one's self-image (Steele, 1988).

Previous studies have identified potential barriers to critical reflection or self-reflection such as time pressures, ego or inflated self-esteem, and "a lack of understanding of the process and its benefits" (Berger & Erzikova, 2019, p. 8; Eurich, 2017; Porter, 2017). Scholars also caution about engaging in healthy self-reflection (*adaptive*) and avoiding harmful thinking (*maladaptive)* (Avolio & Wernsing, 2008). *Adaptive* self-reflection refers to "critical thinking, involving examination and evaluation that results in insights (aha! moments) and learning about the self," while *maladaptive* involves "spending time ruminating what and why things went wrong and never deriving positive lessons learned" (Avolio & Wernsing, 2008; p. 159).

DOI: 10.4324/9781003451709-5

Critical Self-Reflection

Earlier in their careers, some of the Fellows admitted they lacked self-confidence and were hesitant to speak up. Ron Culp explained that people-pleasing was behind this personal weakness:

> In my pursuit of keeping everyone happy, I wouldn't necessarily tell people directly what I was thinking, and as a result, they sometimes inferred I was giving an okay to something that I wasn't entirely on board with. As a result, I would have to come back and clarify my position. They would say, "Oh, we thought that's what you wanted." Eventually, I learned that it was possible to be both direct and nice. But as my wife would confirm, it took a while for me to get there. Today, I can be brutally honest if I think you're off-track or going to get in trouble for something. But I try to do so in a respectful, sometimes self-effacing manner.

Mark Dvorak explained how his reluctance to speak up led his team to make a public mistake by publishing a letter in a national newspaper that was critical of an organization's decision:

> The tone of letter was all wrong. Not sharing my concerns at the 11th hour is to this day, my biggest career regret. One of the subject matter experts we pulled in on the project, and who championed printing the letter, is easily on my most respected list. He is beyond brilliant. I'm thinking it must be the right strategy if he believed in it. In retrospect, I should have spoken up. At the time my gut was shouting "No. Don't do this. It doesn't matter that a lot of work will be wasted if we bag it. It will be wrong. It will be very badly received." I was reading the room and I didn't say something when it still could have changed the outcome. So, the open letter ran. And then we were running to deal with blowback.

His reluctance to speak up could be described as *prosocial silence*, which is associated with altruism or cooperation and courtesy toward others (Van Dyne et al., 2003). Dvorak said he learned an important lesson from the experience:

> It was a very big reminder that I don't do myself or my clients any good if I'm not always challenging assumptions and asking questions. Until the very last moment.

Similarly, Mickey Nall regrets that he didn't initially speak up when assigned to an account with an abusive client:

> It was obvious I was not liked, I was not valued, and I was not appreciated. And the client was very abusive in the first three or four meetings. I was so

taken aback . . . I'm like, okay, I can fix that. . . . I can make you love me, you know, that kind of thing . . .. I did everything I could. She was awful in those settings. And she got worse and worse and more abusive. And I just kind of took it. And if I have one regret, it is that's a minor kind of regret . . . that I didn't just get up and say we quit. We don't want to work with you.

Eventually, Nall did express his concerns to his supervisors who wanted the team to rebid the account when it came up for renewal. He described his frustrations:

I didn't feel listened to. I didn't feel valued on that one account. And so, the funny thing is the person that hated me the most set me free. Because she didn't hire us again. They hired another firm and I wrote her the loveliest – I sent her a massive bouquet, a couple hundred dollar bouquet of flowers with a lovely note that didn't say in the note, it was a pleasure to work with you. It was best of luck for your future and the future of your work and your organization. Wished the organization, not her, you know all the best. And it was nice, but it was, you know, it had nothing to do with her. And damned if I didn't get a thank you note back and, you know, showed it to my people. And they're like, oh, you ended it so classy, Mickey.

Nall said later on when he had the opportunity to lead his own office in Atlanta, he would not tolerate clients that were abusive to their staff. "We don't work that way. If that's the kind of arrangement you want, we need to help you find another agency. And it usually stopped," he said.

Gene Hall reflected on the various risks he took in life that didn't always turn into astounding successes:

Many of the things that I wanted in life were near misses for me. I wanted to play college football. I was too small to play linebacker, which was my high school position. I was too slow to play in the secondary. So that really wasn't an option for me, at least not at Texas A&M, where I knew I wanted to graduate. My FFA experiences had led me to that conclusion. So, I could have played at a small place up north, but I didn't. So that was a near miss. I wanted to be state president of the FFA and here again someone else got that spot. I was a state vice president and – and very glad that I got the opportunity to do that, but I wanted to be a state president. Toward the end of my career, my boss retired. I wanted to be chief operating officer, executive director of the Texas Farm Bureau. I applied for the job and someone else got it and is doing a very good job. So, my career and the experiences that directly led to my career, I have to say, were a series of near misses. But never getting to the top rung doesn't mean they were failures in the aggregate, because each one of them told me things

about myself, told me things about the way I was going about my job . . .
So those were failures in the moment, but I can't look back upon my career
with anything but fondness.

Kena Lewis offered a similar sentiment:

> I know that failure is a learning opportunity. I have learned more from
> instances when I have failed than when I have succeeded. I cannot stress
> that enough to young people – don't take failure as – that you fail, use it as
> a learning opportunity.

Philip Tate said he is inspired by this quote from Theodore Roosevelt,
which is related to crucibles:

> It is not the critic who counts; not the man who points out how the
> strong man stumbles, or where the doer of deeds could have done
> them better. The credit belongs to the man who is actually in the
> arena, whose face is marred by dust and sweat and blood; who strives
> valiantly; who errs, who comes short again and again, because there is
> no effort without error and shortcoming; but who does actually strive
> to do the deeds; who knows great enthusiasms, the great devotions;
> who spends himself in a worthy cause; who at the best knows in the
> end the triumph of high achievement, and who at the worst, if he fails,
> at least fails while daring greatly, so that his place shall never be with
> those cold and timid souls who neither know victory nor defeat.
>
> Theodore Roosevelt
> Speech at the Sorbonne, Paris, April 23, 1910

Anthony D'Angelo recounted an early disappointment in his career that
challenged him:

> So, in my agency days, there was a time when I was among a group of late
> twentysomething, early thirtysomething professionals that were trying to
> move up into agency management. And the agency itself was growing and
> was maturing from being, kind of smaller and led by the original founders
> and learning to say, hey, we've got to incorporate these younger folks into
> the management and bring them along. So, there was a strategic planning
> meeting that was called of a bunch of people, and I was left out of it. And

so, people that I viewed as peers were involved. And I wasn't. And I didn't know whether to be angry or sad or what I could do about it. So, I had a heart to heart talk with the agency president and he was very encouraging to me . . . about my future and also moving into the management ranks when the time is right. He said some things about me that I agreed with and about where I was and some things I didn't agree with. And so, it was a tough lesson.

Rather than become discouraged, D'Angelo chose to work harder, demonstrating his resilience:

I figuratively looked in the mirror and said, "What are you doing and what do you want?" Because you're almost 30 now and you've got to decide at some point if you want to be subject to what happens to you or if you want to drive what happens to you. So, without really working up a formal plan, I decided that I could work harder . . . And so, all of a sudden, I was on the management team and I was getting these really neat assignments and all that sort of stuff. So that tough lesson, but very personally profitable lesson, was – if you have a certain amount of ability, you can get by on that ability for a certain amount of time. But it's not enough. You've got to apply it, right? You've got to challenge yourself.

Overwork and Burnout

However, several Fellows cautioned that public relations practitioners need to be aware of the potential for overworking and burnout, especially when managing major crises. Dr. Dean Kruckeberg referred to it as "a freedom to work yourself to death." Jeremy Burton described the sheer exhaustion he experienced after working 16–18 hour days while managing the crisis at Oral Roberts University:

During that crisis time I did get very wound up. My nerves were shot. I was paranoid. I had trouble sleeping. This trauma persisted for a little more than a year. I finally took a break with my wife. We spent a few days ahead of a work conference together on a beach in Florida. I would spend hours hunting for shells and listening to the rhythm of the waves. There was a moment where my body finally relaxed – where I was able to have some peace. To this day not getting in that mode is something I have to work on because I sometimes get too keyed up. Especially, during these hard crisis times, it's difficult to keep things in perspective.

The European Communication Monitor 2022 report revealed that there are reasons for concern about mental health and wellness for communication professionals. Based on survey results with a sample of 1,672 communication professionals in 43 countries, 66% reported being immersed in their work, and 37% disagreed with the statement "I do not feel used up at the end of a work day" (Zerfass et al., 2022).

Gayle Falkenthal also experienced physical and mental exhaustion after working non-stop for the district attorney's office for more than seven years:

> I absolutely burned myself out, burned to a crisp, burned myself out. I had not taken a day's vacation in all that time. It was a 24-hour, seven day a week job. I pounded myself into the ground. My boss was very happy to let me do it. And every time the County of San Diego said to him, she's going to use it or lose it situation with vacation, he would write me a waiver for them to cash me out so I could stay on the job . . . And I regret it. I regret a lot of those times I have been, you know, so burned out as to not be good company for anybody, not be functional. Which is why I'm so pleased to see the younger generations behind us having viewed and learned those lessons about life balance.

In a related vein, several of the Fellows mentioned that they have struggled with personal health and wellness issues. Mark McClennan discussed his personal battle:

> There is one I haven't solved. I'm morbidly obese. It's significantly impacting my life. I'm on crutches because I can't walk long distances. I look at what chairs I can sit on at business meetings because I don't want to break a chair and fall down (it has happened). It makes traveling tough. In some ways, I am lucky. I come off as the happy fat guy. I also have a loud voice that can dominate a room with my presence, which helps out some. But it's a legitimate concern – it keeps me from doing the things I want to do.

It took a personal health crisis for Ira Yellen to realize the dangers of overworking:

> I knew I had to take some time off from my 12-hour six-day work habit. In hindsight, this among other reasons, led to having open heart bypass surgery. Reality set in, *wait a minute, I could be dead.* I had to accept it was not worth the price. It's not healthy and was selfish, and to my surprise – even my wonderful clients told me it was about time you realized this. I had a great staff who wanted more responsibility, not only to take the load off of me, but for me to give them the power to manage clients and the work. My agency was even more profitable. I started taking more time for me and my wife to travel to the many places around the world we had put off for years.

Yellen said the lesson he learned was "You can't work every day and then take some time off on Sunday and think you are living a healthy and fulfilling life."

At one point in his career, Philip Tate faced a difficult choice. He loved working in sports marketing, but he also wanted to be a good husband and father to his daughters:

> When I finished running the Final Four here in Charlotte, I felt like I was standing at a crossroads. What would I do moving forward? One of my reasons for going to work for Steve Luquire was I admired him as a person and a good role model. He was happily married with two great kids. And I saw a man who spent a lot of time with his family. He went to his son's baseball games. He went to his daughter's cheerleading competitions. He prioritized family. So that's when I decided to take a step away from working in sports all the time, because I was very challenged to find other role models who worked in sports. Think about how sports work. You work long agency hours, 60 plus hours a week, and when are the games? The games are on weeknights and on weekends. When you're single or young married, it's a wonderful place to work. But if you want to be a good parent – one who is present in his children's lives – I don't think you want to be working in sports. If you want to truly give the time and effort required to be a good parent and to be a positive role model, you must be present in your children's lives. So that's when I made the decision to work for an agency that would give me a little more certainty and security.

Tate said he didn't have to fully give up his passion, which was a good compromise:

> I was still able to work with sports clients, but in a different way. It didn't require as much travel and allowed me to work more of a nine-to-five job or as close as you can in the agency business. It was more reasonable and allowed me an opportunity to become a parent my children could look up to.

Even following his career change, Tate had the opportunity to work with the Carolina Panthers, Charlotte 49ers, numerous NCAA championship events, and PGA Tour golf. But more importantly, he was able to spend more quality time with his family.

Geri Evans discussed her tendency to volunteer for a lot of worthy causes, but she has more recently realized her limitations:

> When one's calendar is filled to capacity and overflowing, as most are, there is no room for the unexpected – the 5–10% more that seems to come

along almost daily. That can be frustrating, exhausting, and unsustainable. Something gets short-changed. I truly wished I had learned this earlier in my career and life because now that I practice this (most of the time) an unexpected phone call or a friend's need for help is a joy not "another thing to add to the list."

Other Personal Struggles

Whereas some Fellows struggled with overwork and burnout, others battled internal challenges such as self-confidence, grief, perfectionism, a desire for control, or a lack of openness to other perspectives. For some, it was physical appearance that led to some restrictions on opportunities that were presented. Evans put this focus on physical appearance into perspective:

> It is something that I've always been keenly aware of (because I battled weight throughout my life) and it's a story that I have been able to turn into something I can use to help others. It is all about where we place value as a society and how we acknowledge it and move beyond it. At age 40, I had a gastric bypass. Within a year, I had lost almost 100 pounds. What struck me continuously is the fact that though I was the same person inside with the same strengths and weaknesses, many new opportunities were open to me because I was thinner. And I wanted to shout, "Wait a minute! Just because I'm thinner, now I'm allowed to do all of the things I knew I could do when I was not thin?" Wow, makes me wonder sometimes about where we place our values and how we make judgments before we get to know someone. It's another serious and real example of the old adage, "Don't judge a book by its cover."

Col. Christian Patterson faced multiple challenges while deployed to Afghanistan to serve as a commander of a public affairs unit. His faith carried him through these tough times and illustrates the power of affirming identity anchors, backgrounding negative feelings, and focusing on the positive to achieve resilience (Buzzanell, 2010). As Patterson explained:

> I had some tremendous challenges with leading a few members of my team who just did not want to cooperate and were very unruly and made an already difficult situation much harder than what it had to be. And so sometimes as a leader, you will have people that will just come after you for any reason, unfortunately. I relied heavily on my faith while we were in country.

Patterson said the reality of war and the death of fellow soldiers made this a very stressful time:

> What really compounded the challenges present within my unit was what was going on around us in theater. We were at Bagram Airfield, which had

one street and the airfield. The name of the street was Disney Drive and it was a mile long. During the deployment, we lost a lot of soldiers during combat operations. There were several weeks where every week we would have a fallen soldier ceremony. Humvees with flag draped coffins in the back would move slowly from one end of Disney to the other. Unit members sat on both sides of the coffin and were there to load the fallen onto a C-17 Globemaster III aircraft to be flown back to the States. And so, when you had that type of thing going on, in addition to difficult soldiers, it was tough.

It's important to stress that backgrounding negative feelings "is a conscious decision to acknowledge that one has the legitimate right to feel anger or loss in certain ways," especially in times of war and death, but "these feelings are counterproductive to more important goals" (Buzzanell, 2010, p. 9). For Patterson, he had a mission and troops to lead. His faith served as an identity anchor to help him through those difficult days (Buzzanell, 2010):

And I just remember getting off of work most nights around 11:15, walking to my B-hut (Barracks Hut), and before I walked in with all the people that I lived with, I would sit in a large, empty sewer pipe that was above the ground and I would pray for probably 10, 15 minutes. That helped me to be able to walk into my B-Hut and actually be strong and resilient for the people that I lived with because they had problems, too.

Patterson said the experiences helped him to develop patience and resilience. Those character strengths eventually resulted in a significant promotion:

For Army public affairs officers, it's extremely difficult to make full bird Colonel, especially if you're in the National Guard or the Army Reserve. The selection rates are extremely low. I had been a lieutenant colonel since May 2, 2013, and had given up hope. But I kept on trying. I didn't give up . . . And so in the matter of weeks, God made a move that was better than any plan I could ever come up with. I had been trying to come up with some things. But he basically said, you can plan all you want to, but it's not going to be as good as what I have coming . . . It is extremely historic. I will be the first black commander in the history of ERDC [U.S. Army Engineer Research and Development Center], which dates back to 1927 when it was the Waterways Experiment Station. I will also be the first non-engineer commander, and then I will be the first reservist commander. So, it has been life changing.

There are other internal personal struggles. Mark Dvorak shared his tendency to plan and aim for perfection earlier in his career. However, an important shift in life perspective came after battling stage four – or metastatic – cancer:

> If I could go back to when I was 25, when I worried about everything and everything had to be perfect. And I believed I had to be great at everything... and at all times. Worried constantly about the "what's next" and not making a single mistake. Cancer gave me tremendous clarity. None of us is perfect. In fact, we are not going to excel in every area of anything – particularly our careers. Instead of beating yourself up about those things, use the time and energy instead to get clarity about your passions and skills. And in particular, where do they meet? In your day job, in your community or anywhere else, that's where a content and fulfilled life begins and where anxiety dissipates. This realization has done more to bring me peace and confidence than any single activity or event. When you operate from a place of authenticity like this, you will be amazed at the impact you make.

Dvorak is currently serving as the chair of the PRSA Board of Ethics & Professional Standards.

In a similar vein to Dvorak's personal struggle for perfection, Jeremy Burton described his battle for control:

> Professionally – one of the things that's a challenge for me is letting go of control. I learned early in life that if I could control it, I could achieve it. Having that posture is not always good. Sometimes you have to let go and you have to give up things in order to do your job the best. The part of me that wants to control is a shadow of myself that I still often fight with. This was a struggle for me as a young professional and is for other young professionals I have known. Everyone wants to be the vice president. Everyone wants to be the president. Everyone wants to grow quickly and begin to control what their department does based on their knowledge. There can be a lack of self-awareness in ways they need to grow to take that next step in their career. As I grew in title and scope, projects or initiatives become your "baby." If your superiors come and take away your "baby," for any reason, you have to grieve that loss of control. I've experienced these situations a number of times in my career and I haven't always handled them well. In those moments I've had to learn humility and not think too highly of myself.

Mary Deming Barber says her personal vice is stubbornness. She described this personal struggle:

> Even though I talk about how I listen to people, I like to collaborate, I like to try to find the solution, sometimes on certain issues and certain concerns

I know I'm right. And it doesn't matter what you say to me. I know I'm right. And I think that can be a challenge. Especially when you're dealing with a civic issue or a social issue. Because I believe that on those issues, it's really important to keep an open mind and to always listen. And sometimes, like all of us, I think I find myself thinking now I know what I believe on this and it doesn't really matter what you say to me, because I'm right.

Barber discussed how she tries to overcome this vice:

> I remind myself that oh, wait. You're being stubborn. I do I talk to myself, and I tell myself that I'm being stubborn and I need to slow down. It's usually because I'm going too quickly. I have too much on my plate. And I need to just kind of slow down and take a couple breaths and realize that the other person has a point too. And, okay, I heard you and then realize that maybe we can come to some sort of solution. But it's usually just taking those breaths and slowing down.

Failures and Regrets

Of course, some of the Fellows did not always live up to their personal ideals. Rebecca Villarreal described a moment when she took out her frustrations on her administrative assistant at the time:

> At one point when I got a new boss and my career was getting more demanding and challenges were becoming harder. I wouldn't say I took it out on her, but I remember getting on to her about something important that she knew how to do and had been responsible for overseeing for the past few years. I pretty much berated her. I didn't punish her. I didn't write her up. It wasn't anything to that extent. It was more like a disappointment that I was sharing, but also a frustration. And it really hit her hard. And she was never the same team player after that. That all really weighed on her. And I regretted doing it. I regretted saying it. And the bigger regret is that she actually did move into another position.

Villarreal said she has tried to make amends with her former employee:

> I see her occasionally and I talk to her. I'm friendly to her. I would send her cards on her birthday and I would text her because I just really wanted her to know I care about her and I am sorry. And maybe I didn't apologize enough to her, but you just can't take out your frustrations and stress on anyone else like family or coworkers. You just have to work through it. That's one regret I have.

Geri Evans also discussed a personal regret early in her career:

> I didn't understand my value. I didn't speak up for myself nearly as often as I should have. I was timid about asking for what I needed.

She later did advocate for herself and ended up resigning a job that she enjoyed when her supervisor was unwilling to acknowledge her contributions.

> I felt it was time for a raise. I felt it was time for recognition of what I had contributed. I felt it was time for an opportunity to take a deep breath then use my new self-confidence and awareness, and find a place where I could use my talents and succeed. I did.

By engaging in critical reflection, the Fellows were able to learn from crucible experiences and become aware of their personal strengths and weaknesses (Kernis, 2003). It's important that young professionals who may look to these public relations leaders as role models realize that their paths to success involved many setbacks, obstacles, and disappointments. Their successes came due to persistence, resilience, and hard work.

Berger and Erzikova (2019) developed a six-step process for engaging in personal reflection:

1. **Make time for SR**. It's too important to be too busy . . . Walking, exercising, tending the garden, riding to work, reading books, writing in a diary – choose an approach that works best for you.
2. **Create the "right" mindset**. Like *putting on a game face*, in SR we must create a mental space where SR fills the foreground . . .
3. **Be self-honest and balance your assessment** . . . First, don't let ego overpower your self-critique and, second, don't let self-criticism (rumination) lead to inaction or loss of confidence.
4. **Formulate actions** based on your assessment and evaluation. Calendar them. Consider discussing them with a mentor or colleague.
5. **Carry out actions**. Be professional, timely, and authentic. Rehearsing the actions to test and refine them may be useful.
6. **Self-reflect on the outcomes** and renew the cycle. Writing things down may help at this point. Over time, this process becomes routine (p. 16).

Berger and Erzikova (2019) also provided some sample questions that can be used to engage in the critical reflection process such as "How might others react to your proposed words or actions? What values would your actions (or words) express?" or "How would you assess the impact of your behavior on others?" (p. 16).

Questions to Consider

1. Which of these reflections did you find to be most relevant to your own life and why?
2. One of the more common struggles among the Fellows was a tendency toward overworking and burnout. What can public relations practitioners do to prevent this in their own lives?
3. How difficult is it for you to engage in critical reflection when you are confronting personal weaknesses? Why do you think this is necessary for leaders to address these issues?
4. Which of the strategies (e.g., crafting normalcy, affirming identity anchors, maintaining and using communication networks, putting alternative logics to work, and downplaying negative feelings while foregrounding positive emotions) do you find effective for achieving resilience when faced with challenges?

References

Avolio, B. J., & Wernsing, T. S. (2008). Practicing authentic leadership. In S. J. Lopez (Ed.), *Positive psychology: Exploring the best in people* (Vol. 4, pp. 147–165). Greenwood Publishing Group.

Berger, B. K., & Erzikova, E. (2019). Self-reflection in public relations leaders: A study of its practice and value in Russia and North America, *Public Relations Journal, 13*(1), 1–22.

Buzzanell, P. M. (2010). Resilience: Talking, resisting and imagining new normalcies into being. *Journal of Communication, 60*, 1–14.

Byrne, A., Crossan, M., & Seijts, G. (2018). The development of leader character through crucible moments. *Journal of Management Education, 42*(2), 265–293.

Chance, N. L. (2021). A phenomenological inquiry into the influence of crucible experiences on the leadership development of Black women in higher education senior leadership. *Educational Management Administration & Leadership, 49*(4), 601–623.

Duhachek, A. (2005). Coping: A multidimensional, hierarchical framework of responses to stressful consumption episodes. *Journal of Consumer Research, 32*(1), 41–53.

Eurich, T. (2017). *Insight.* Crown Business.

Kernis, M. H. (2003). Toward a conceptualization of optimal self-esteem. *Psychological Inquiry, 14*, 1–26.

Porter, J. (2017, March). Why you should make time for self-reflection (even if you hate doing it). *Harvard Business Review.* https://hbr.org/2017/03/why-you-should-make-time-for-self-reflection-even-if-you-hate-doing-it

Steele, C. M. (1988). The psychology of self-affirmation. Sustaining integrity of the self. In L. Berkowitz (Ed.), *Advances in experimental social psychology* (Vol. 21, pp. 261–302). Academic.

Van Dyne, L., Ang, S., & Botero, I. C. (2003). Conceptualizing employee silence and employee voice as multidimensional constructs. *Journal of Management Studies, 40*(6), 1359–1392.

Zerfass, A., Moreno, A., Tench, R., Verčič, D., & Buhmann, A. (2022). *European Communication Monitor.* www.communicationmonitor.eu/2022/07/07/ecm-european-communication-monitor-2022/

6 Phronesis – Practical Wisdom and Resilience

Introduction

Phronesis, or practical wisdom, is developed through life experiences such as crucibles (Hursthouse, 1999). It is associated with human flourishing or *eudaimonia* (Borden, 2019; Hursthouse, 1999). As Borden (2019) wrote, "The virtuous agent becomes gradually more expert at doing the right thing using the moral knowledge gained from her embedded experiences; she does the right thing for its own sake and takes pleasure in doing so" (Cunningham, 1999, p. 182). She pointed out that Aristotle's notion of flourishing is grounded in the principles of a "shared life," which is consistent with the idea of a "reciprocal nature of social influence" that transforms and shapes leaders (Borden, 2019; Colby & Damon, 1992, p. 14). Over the years, family members, friends, mentors, and colleagues "challenged, prodded, supplied information, asked questions, gave feedback, and otherwise supported the exemplar's" growth and development of "moral vision" (Colby & Damon, 1992, p. 295). Consistent with the reciprocal nature, others also looked to the exemplars for inspiration and direction, and then their support helped the exemplars grow and progress (Colby & Damon, 1992).

Moral development begins in our childhood, primarily based on interactions with our parents, which has been referred to as *primary socialization* (Berger & Luckmann, 1967). Several of the Fellows mentioned early lessons that they learned from their parents or legal guardians, which led to moral awareness. These childhood and adolescent experiences were so impactful because their parents and grandparents modeled virtuous behavior rather than simply preaching about it (Vardeman & Schauster, 2021). The next developmental stage is identification, when someone adopts good behavior in order to maintain relationships with another person or group (Kelman, 1961), a process referred to as *secondary socialization* (Berger & Luckmann, 1967). In later stages of moral development, *social norms* influence behavior, which refers to "rules and standards that are understood by members of a group and that guide and/or constrain social behavior without the force of laws" (Cialdini & Trost, 1998, p. 152), such as industry codes of ethics. Also, *descriptive*

DOI: 10.4324/9781003451709-6

norms can be influential, which refers to what is actually done in practice and motivates us to imitate the behavior of those who achieve various forms of success (Cialdini & Trost, 1998). As Bandura (2001) wrote, "people are motivated by the successes of others who are similar to themselves but are discouraged from pursuing courses of behavior that they have seen often result in adverse consequences" (p. 274). All of this ties into the core focus of this study of exemplars as role models.

Generosity

Consistent with the concept of *primary socialization*, Dr. Amiso George discussed how she learned about the importance of generosity from her father:

> My dad always used to say the pie is big enough. You can't eat the entire pie by yourself, and we're not gonna take it with us. We will not take it with us. So, I am a great believer in 'Do unto others as you would have them do unto you.'

But consistent with Aristotle's Golden Mean, her generosity is limited:

> I have family members, extended family members who would ask me for one thing or the other and I give, but then it gets to a point where I can't give any more because then I wouldn't be able to have enough for myself. And I tell them you know what, I have helped for so long. I just can't anymore. And that's – it's not coming from a place of weakness. It's simply coming from a place of self-preservation and I have helped you a lot and I expect you should take from there and move on.

Dr. Debra Miller recalls words of wisdom from her grandmother regarding the importance of making an impact:

> My Bahamian Haitian grandmother used to often say, "You don't want to be a stick in the mud," after I would share a recent accomplishment or what I had done in school that day beginning in first grade. Every time I would ask her, "what does that mean, Gramma?" She would very softly say, "You're a smart girl, think about it, the answer will come to you." Well, I thought about it for many years, and she eventually took the answer to her grave. One day, the meaning came to me in a series of questions. What is a stick in the mud, really? Just a stick in the mud. You can either break it or leave it there until it totally disappears over time. I think she was trying to challenge and encourage me to be the person actually placing the stick in the mud. That is a person who controls her own destiny, a leader and someone whose life has meaning. In her own way Gramma was asking

Figure 6.1 Margaret Ann Hennen (on the right) holds one of the bears that she hand-knitted. She is with a family friend, Margaret Arazi, an avid bear knitter at age 98.

me to define my purpose. Maybe she was using the illustration to challenge and encourage me to make the world better for myself and for others. She expected me to do all that I could to make my life better than hers. It was her way of saying you have to do something important every day to do that. You can't stand still, stop thinking, doing, working and dreaming. You can't just exist because you will become a stick in the mud. No one will know you were on this earth. I thank her every day for that challenge as I continuously strive to make sure that my contribution to the world is unique and powerful. I refuse to be a stick in the mud.

Margaret Ann Hennen learned about generosity and making an impact from her parents, who would take food to people in need in their community. More recently, she has been involved with an organization for nearly 20 years that provides hand-knitted bears to children in Africa:

This community has knit hundreds of thousands of bears that have been sent to primarily African countries, primarily South Africa. As I'm sure you know, AIDS in South Africa is horrendous. There are missing genera-tions and these kids have nothing. And so, this bear becomes very impor-tant. And then she [the founder] sews a heart on the bear and puts a little tag on it. The tag says with love and the knitter signs their name . . . these bears bring comfort. They bring love.

Notice in these personal anecdotes focused on generosity and making impact-specific references to themes associated with *communion* or expressions of "altruism, sympathy, care, and helping others in need" (McAdams et al., 1996, p. 350), demonstrating a desire on the part of several of the Fellows to "leave the world a better place than they found it."

Resilience

As previously mentioned, resilience is an essential characteristic of the Fellows that allowed them to thrive when faced with crucibles. Gayle Falkenthal learned resilience by watching her mother take over the family business, a motorcycle repair shop, when her father died at a young age. To some degree, it appears her mother was able to craft some degree of normalcy by maintaining "the mundane, the regularities in life that previously would have gone unnoticed" (Buzzanell, 2010, p. 3). As Falkenthal explained:

> Resilience is such an important commodity in life. We're all going to suffer things that are unfair or unexpected, and the ability to just tell yourself to hang on and move forward is a real asset. It doesn't seem like a big thing until you must reach for it and really ride it hard to get through those tough things in life. It was modeled for me very well by my family . . . I regret not having more conversations with my mother about her life and how that went and how she did it. But I do think I absorbed the knowledge by observing her actions, by her survival. Watching her accomplish this by a woman who was 50-ish . . . who was educated in the '50s and '60s, suddenly having to step up. I'm sure never in a million years did she think she'd have to call upon herself to do this. You see what comes from just hanging in there. Sometimes I think life's great accomplishment is you just hung in there.

Resilience refers to ability to cope successfully when faced with changes, various forms of adversity or risk (Stewart et al., 1997), or the "ability to resist being overwhelmed or defined by loss or negative experiences" (Plaisance, 2014, p. 176). Resilient people "are able to *assimilate* loss into their existing self-narratives in a way that it does not radically undermine the central themes of their life stories and, indeed, may even affirm them" (Neimeyer, 2006, p. 71). Chance (2021) argued "that leadership development results from resilience, and the cost of resilience is lived adversity" (e.g., crucibles) (p. 617). Some of the core leadership skills that can be developed through crucibles include "emotional intelligence, focus/motivation, self-discipline, faith/hope, self-esteem and commitment" (Chance, 2021, p. 619). Related to resilience is hardiness – a trait described as "a pattern of attitudes and strategies that together facilitate turning stressful circumstances from potential disasters into growth opportunities" (Maddi, 2013, p. 8).

Honesty

Colonel Christian Patterson recalls an important lesson on virtues from his high school English teacher, which served as a *memorable message* (i.e., moral directive):

> One of the lessons that she taught me, and I remember it to this day and will never forget it, is do not lie. Do not fudge the truth. She asked me a question in class one day and I knew that it wasn't the full truth. And so, the bell rang and I got on the opposite end of the hallway after I left her class. And so literally, about 30 seconds after I left with all these kids in the hallway, I hear somebody yell, "Christian Patterson. Why did you lie to me?" All of the kids froze in their tracks as if they were in trouble and it was a huge deal. And so, I've always remembered that. And that lesson kind of morphed into my career in public relations because we deal in truth. As a matter of fact, the Defense Information School's motto is *strength through truth*. It's shortened name is DINFOS, and it is located at Fort Meade, Maryland.

Civility

Anthony D'Angelo had to deal with division while serving in various leadership roles. He discussed the principles that guided him in addressing difficult situations:

> In a lot of those tough situations, I think you have to go back to first principles. And I think the first principles for us are the code of ethics and your own moral compass, your own sense of your own values and your own mission in the world. And if you're true to those things, you can disagree, hopefully without being disagreeable. But we live in a world, as you certainly know, that is increasingly polarized and, thanks to social media, not given to carefully considered thought or nuance. I think it falls to PR professionals to employ the discipline and patience it requires to communicate with empathy, to find common ground, to stay engaged until the proverbial 'third solution' is reached thanks to true collaboration.

D'Angelo has since assisted with the development of the Voices4Everyone initiative within PRSA, which focuses on diversity and inclusion, countering mis- and disinformation, and promoting civility and civic engagement.

Sacrifice

For Ron Culp, a lesson in his parents' selflessness and sacrifice was revealed to him later as an adult. When he visited a college friend who went into insurance sales, he gave Culp a tour of the massive records archive of Meridian Mutual. He pulled Culp's insurance file folder, which contained a paragraph about his parents' financial status:

> That was the first time in my life I discovered my parents were not as well off as I had assumed my entire life. From childhood through college, everything I wanted to do, they somehow found the energy and the money and debt that it took to do it. So, I was surprised when I graduated from college, was unemployed and moved to Indianapolis and needed to pay for the deposit and first month's rent. Of course, I called mom and dad. Their response was, "Right now, it's kind of tight. Can you perhaps take out a loan or something?" That confirmed what was in the insurance report. At that very moment I said, "I am going to work my ass off and I want to – if I need to, take care of them or whatever," but I never really had to do as much as they did for me. They somehow made ends meet. But I did make sure that they didn't pay for dinner when we occasionally got together. I remain inspired today about those simpler times when my parents were able to raise four kids on so little money.

Power of Listening

A couple of the Fellows mentioned how they have learned to listen more after spending much of their careers providing counsel to others. As a senior professional and founder of his family business, Three Box Strategic Communications, Blake Lewis has learned to listen more and allow younger professionals to make decisions:

> It used to be spending a lot of time telling people – based upon my experiences – what they should do, and now, when somebody comes to me, whether I think that they have the innate ability to come up with the answer or not, they ask the question, and there's only one right answer: "What do you think? What do you think is the right way to solve this problem? What is the right way to capitalize on this opportunity?" Because the answer to that question then informs the route you want to take.

Listening provided Ann Barkelew with a solution to help employees impacted by job losses when her employer Munsingwear had to close a plant. As she explained:

> And when I went in – went up there, I said, you know, we have to ask the employees what they think. You know, explain – here's the problem. Lay

it out for them. Be honest with them . . . We said to the employees, "What can we do to help this be easier for you and your families?" And I remember this one woman said to me, "Give us our sewing machines." She said, "I could really run a good business doing alterations and making things for people, but I don't have that kind of sewing machine." And we bought so much goodwill by giving the sewing machines – because what were we going to do with all these extra sewing machines, right?

Advice on Speaking Up

The Fellows also learned about the importance of speaking up and contributing. As Dr. Debra Miller said:

I believe that having an informed opinion and the confidence to share it is a "superpower" all critical strategic communicators should possess. I learned the power of speaking up when I learned about the power of the written word early in my life and career. I became more confident in sharing my views with others once I read Maya Angelou's words " *I've learned that people will forget what you said, people will forget what you did, but people will never forget how you made them feel.*" These words are etched in my brain and have become part of my DNA. One must be prepared before you speak which means knowing what you are talking about before you open your mouth. Asking questions for clarity and understanding can help position you to make knowledgeable and impactful comments and recommendations. There have been times when my recommendations or position on an issue or an action have been challenged, but I never take it personally. You have to stand firm in what you know and what you bring to the table, regardless of where the table is.

She also stressed the importance of listening before speaking up:

I take great pride in having developed a reputation for being a thoughtful, strategic critical thinker. I intentionally spend more time listening and observing the behavior of others before I speak. When I do speak, I bring an informed authenticity in my words. Sometimes it's a statement, other times it's a question. As a C-suite advisor my role has been to bring you the good, the bad and the ugly. In other words, educate, invigorate, solve problems and bring solutions and results to the table. If you can do that, you'll always have a seat at the table. And sometimes silence can be even more powerful.

However, Kelly Davis received some wise counsel from a boss about improving her delivery when counseling a client:

She just looked at me and she said, "Kelly, tone matters, the tone of voice." And I was there and I was trying to explain to her my philosophy and what they wanted me to do, which I thought was not ethical. And she was like, "But sometimes it's how you say it and how you get it across in the tone of voice you're using. That is just as important as the information that you're trying to convey." And I realize that. And so, I think about that. So, I just I hear her saying that so many times. Tone matters. Tone matters.

Margaret Ann Hennen provided some wisdom about speaking up to report unprofessional behavior. She described a traumatic incident early in her career:

> I was in a meeting with a group of people probably 10 people . . . And right at the end of the meeting, this person who was essentially a salesperson had been with the company many, many years. He said something – I would tell you if I could remember what it was, but it was demeaning not just to me but to all women in business. And I was flabbergasted by this. I went back to my office and thought about it for a minute. I thought no, I'm not going to let this slide. I can't. I have to respect myself. I have to work for that respect.

Hennen handled the issue in a professional manner. As she explained:

> I sat down and wrote what had happened leaving out all emotion, strictly the facts. Here's what happened. And I sent it to the head of HR. He called me and asked, "Are you okay if I take and talk to a couple of the other people who were in the meeting?" I said, "Of course." He called me back and said, "I talked to two or three people." He told me who they were and he said their stories are almost verbatim your story. And that's when I learned here's the wisdom part – in a business context, check your emotion at the door and stick to the facts.

The company leadership called another meeting and the salesman publicly apologized to Hennen.

Teamwork and Collaboration

While much of the focus of the Fellows' stories has been on individual accomplishments, over time, Anthony D'Angelo has learned the importance of teamwork and collaboration:

> I learned at some point that it's not just individual effort that is rewarded, but it's a different kind of reward if you've been able to collaborate with a team. And those rewards are more satisfying and far-reaching, and they have residual effects so you remember them a lot longer.

Similarly, Blake Lewis had this to say, "being surrounded and supported by other people who are as capable or, even better, more capable than you is a wise thing to do."

Hennen described how important it is to build and maintain relationships with your colleagues. She made a concerted effort to do so:

> I spent a lot of time in the halls rather than at my desk throughout my career, because that's where I developed relationships with people. And I got a ton of work done walking around in those halls recruiting people to be involved with community events. And just getting to know our employees on a more personal level. You can't in a crisis try to form those relationships. In my opinion, you need to form relationships during periods of calm and call upon them in periods of crisis.

Role of Mentors and Advocates

Tying back to the concept of the *reciprocal nature of social influence*, the Fellows advanced in their careers due to mentors and supervisors who encouraged them to aspire higher – to seek that promotion, to pursue accreditation or advanced degrees, or to take on bigger challenges. As Barbara Burfeind explained:

> Lt Col. Bob (Hastings) was the department head. And Major Dave Medaris was my boss, my supervisor. They were teaching APR classes . . . and they rounded up several of us and said, you all need to do this. And I'm like, I just got here. I need to get my feet on the ground. I need six months. And Major Medaris is like, "No, I know the Navy. We'll be lucky if you're here two years." And I'm like, no, I'll do the full tour – three years . . . He goes, "If you don't start this now, you're not going to do it." And I'm like, okay. So, I started doing the classes with them . . . and in 2000 got my APR, but it was because of them pushing. So, when people get upset about people pushing them, sometimes that's what you need. You don't know what you need sometimes, and they see something in you that you don't see.

Similarly, Mary Deming Barber discussed how she provided that push to a young professional she was mentoring through a relationship established through the PRSA College of Fellows mentorship program. As Barber explained, the young woman was a recent college graduate looking for her first job opportunity:

> I knew any number of people in the city that she was moving to who I could send her to, and several opportunities. But she really needed to branch out on her own and find those opportunities – on her own

meet the people, build the relationships. So that I felt that she needed that growing experience. And she was also extremely self-conscious and didn't think that she could go meet these people because the people I was mentioning were so important if you were a 22-year-old student. It may seem not kind, but I told her I said, "This person is going to be at this location at this time. So, listen to him speak and go introduce yourself." And she said, "Oh, I can't do that." And I said, "That's how it has to happen."

The young woman ended up introducing herself to the speaker, which resulted in a two-hour meeting. Barber said her protégé built her confidence through this experience:

We have talked about that experience numerous times. And she credits that with being a turning point for her career also that she realized that she had the confidence to reach out to those people. And from that point on, they [her family] moved several times after that and she would say, "Do you know anybody in this community" kind of thing? And I would say, "Yes, I know three people." And she'd say, "Okay. Just give me their names. I'll call them." And it was a turning point.

Prior research has identified the roles of *instrumental support* and *psychosocial* in the context of mentoring relationships (Martinelli & Erzikova, 2016). *Instrumental* support can refer to mentors providing "protection, coaching, challenging assignments, career planning advice, sponsorship in the organization and a network of social connections" (Berger et al., 2009, p. 14). *Psychosocial* support for the protégé can be offered "through a mentor's friendship, counseling, acceptance and con-firmation of work, and role modeling of expected values and behaviors" (Berger et al., 2009, p. 15).

Barkelew received that necessary support when seeking counsel from her mentor Pat Jackson regarding whether or not to make the transition to corpo-rate public relations from the public education sector:

When I called Patrick Jackson and said, you know, "They've offered me this opportunity. You know, what do you think? Do you think I could do it?" And I can remember him saying, "You got to do it. You've got to do it. You've got to show them that people coming out of the public sector are just as good, just as professional in public relations as people in the corporate world." And that was at that point in time, that was a big step. There weren't a lot of people moving from public sector public relations into corporate America. They all sort of were coming up through the ranks of corporate America.

Figure 6.2 Stacey Smith with Pat Jackson, her mentor, colleague, and husband.

Stacey Smith's life was changed when she met Pat Jackson while in college:

> It was my senior year, in my senior cases class, that I first met Pat. He showed up to talk to us (as he did at many colleges and universities across the U.S. the year he was president of PRSA). He was in town to do a day-long seminar for the local chapter – something he also did all year to recruit new and invigorate current PRSA members. (I believe the count was over 300 presentations that year alone!) I had decided by that time that if PR was just about working with the media and writing news releases, I wasn't longing for the profession. But Pat had an entirely different take on what our role was, and what we were there to do. His focus was on stakeholder *behaviors* – understanding them, motivating them, changing them by using behavioral science theories and strategies to make a

difference in people's lives, both with internal and external stakeholders. We had the skills and ability to make change in this world. Now *that* was what I wanted to do. We didn't call it social change at the time, but that was exactly what he was talking about. Not only did Pat make me want to stay in PR . . . he made me want to work with Pat's firm! I dogged him until they hired me. There were many professionals over the years that did the same. They had the same "aha" moment and wanted to work with Pat and other members of Jackson Jackson & Wagner. Many are on the cusp of retiring now, but we have all continued to educate others about the true value of public relations and spread the PR gospel according to Pat, recognizing his important contributions to the public relations profession.

Smith not only became an employee at Pat's firm, Jackson Jackson & Wagner, but later they married. She discussed his major influence on the public relations profession starting in 1977 editing *pr reporter* which, under his leadership, became the leading industry thought piece. He remained one of the most sought-after speakers about professional practice both nationally and internationally, until his death in 2001.

Pat would have a slot every year at PRSA's national conference. Sometime early in the year, PRSA staff would call our offices and say, "We have reserved Pat two sessions, each an hour and a half on two different days. What does he want to speak about this year?" They would book the largest room for him because when Pat was going to speak, *everybody* – seasoned and new practitioners – showed up. People would sit on the floor, on the stairs, in the back – people would stand outside the door fighting for a way in. His session was not to be missed – both sessions, every single time. His ability to rivet people to their chair, teach, entertain, and motivate was consistent every time they heard him speak, which was exactly what happened to me every time I heard him. We always pitied the poor folk who were presenting simultaneously! It isn't the same, but there is a Pat Jackson website www.patrickjacksonpr.com that has videos, articles and more. His content is as relevant today as it was then – maybe even more so, given the nature of our society at present.

Learning through Observation

Wisdom also comes from observing your surroundings. Mickey Nall describes the moment he realized his office was lacking diversity:

I was interviewing the top three candidates in my office, looking out in the PR area of the office, I had blonde, stereotypical sorority sisters. I swear to god, every employee I had looked alike, sounded alike, obviously came from a nice upper middle class family, who was supporting her because her wardrobe was so phenomenal. But – and it clicked. It was just the weirdest thing. It just clicked. So, I get up and go over to my account director, who's a blonde, sorority member alumnae. And I'm like "what's going on here? How many resumes did we get? You know, everyone looks alike." Where's – and I didn't use the term diversity. "Where are the young men, where are African Americans?" . . . Atlanta's an African American city. And so, she was like, "Mickey, you can't do that. Really, Mickey, you can't do that. I've gone through the resumes. These resumes I've given you are, you know, the top three candidates." And I went, "Well, let's do this. Give me the pile of resumes. Let me go through them."

Nall then took concerted actions to increase the diversity of his job applicants:

And that led to – I became in North America per capita, the most diverse office in the Ogilvy section at that time. I went over to Morehouse and to Spelman there and started internship programs for African American PR majors to come into Ogilvy. And again, I became the most diverse department. I hired the first Asian American account executive. I hired two young Hispanic women. And literally New York, because at this point, the whole company was trying to become more diverse, New York was calling . . . and they're like, we need you to teach us how to do this. And I was like, people, it wasn't hard. Look at the universities in your marketplace and just reach out. Go make a speech. You'll see.

Fellows as Mentors

As mentors and professors to young professionals, Fellows often have the opportunity to provide wise counsel to young professionals. Ron Culp shared a time when a young woman was considering whether or not to take a job that paid 65% more than her current job. He recounted their conversation:

"You know, what you are doing is important to your agency. As somebody who once ran an agency and someone who worked in a few corporations, I can tell you really like your current job. So, if you love your job, you stay in your job." So, she said, "What do we do?" And I said, "You described your boss as someone very much like me. If that is even remotely true, go talk it out with him." "You can do that?" I said, "Yeah, today you can. Ten years ago, and definitely twenty years ago, you'd have been considered a traitor for even interviewing elsewhere. But today, no, it is a new, talent-focused world. And they don't want to lose you. So go talk it out." She went back to candidly discuss the situation with her boss. She called me later and said, "I did. I was a nervous wreck." The boss told her, "Don't do anything for the next two days if you can buy time." In less than 24 hours – in fact, the next morning, she got a call from her boss – they matched the salary! And she is happy . . . a place that life is working for her and her children and her lifestyle that she dearly loves, and clients she also loves – and now she's getting richly rewarded for it, beyond what she thought was possible – beyond what I thought was possible, quite frankly.

These examples of wisdom and advice demonstrate how *phronesis* or practical wisdom is developed through experiences and the *reciprocal nature of social influence*. Fortunately, many Fellows are willing to share that wisdom with the next generation of public relations professionals.

Questions to Consider

1. What kernels of wisdom have you gleaned from your own personal experiences or interactions?
2. Which piece of advice or wisdom shared by the Fellows did you find most impactful for you personally and why?
3. Who are the most influential mentors in your life and what advice have they provided that has been most beneficial to you?

References

Bandura, A. (2001). Social cognitive theory of mass communication. *Media Psychology*, *3*(3), 265–299. https://doi.org/10.1207/S1532785XMEP0303_03

Berger, B. K., Meng, J., & Heyman, W. (2009, March 11–14). *Role modeling in public relations: The influence of role models and mentors on leadership beliefs and qualities* [Conference Presentation]. International Public Relations Research Conference, Miami, FL, United States.

Berger, P. L., & Luckmann, T. (1967). *The social construction of reality*. Doubleday.

Borden, S. L. (2019). Virtue ethics & media. In P. L. Plaisance (Ed.), *Communication and media ethics* (pp. 171–190). Walter de Gruyter.

Buzzanell, P. M. (2010). Resilience: Talking, resisting and imagining new normalcies into being. *Journal of Communication*, *60*, 1–14.

Chance, N. L. (2021). A phenomenological inquiry into the influence of crucible experiences on the leadership development of Black women in higher education senior leadership. *Educational Management Administration & Leadership*, *49*(4), 601–623.

Cialdini, R. B., & Trost, M. R. (1998). Social influence, social norms, conformity, and compliance. In S. T. Fiske, D. T. Gilbert, & G. Lindzey (Eds.), *The handbook of social psychology* (Vol. 2, pp. 151–192). Oxford University Press.

Colby, A., & Damon, W. (1992). *Some do care: Contemporary lives of moral commitment*. MacMillan, Inc.

Cunningham, S. B. (1999). Getting it right: Aristotle's "golden mean" as theory deterioration. *Journal of Mass Media Ethics*, *14*, 5–15.

Hursthouse, R. (1999). *On virtue ethics*. Oxford University Press.

Kelman, H. C. (1961). Processes of opinion change. *The Public Opinion Quarterly*, *25*(1), 57–78.

Maddi, S. R. (2013). *Hardiness*. Springer.

Martinelli, D., & Erzikova, E. (2016). *Mentoring research and best practices white paper*. http://plankcenter.ua.edu/wpcontent/uploads/2017/07/Mentoring.final_.10.19.16.pdf

McAdams, D. P., Hoffman, B. J., Mansfield, E. D., & Day, R. (1996). Themes of Agency and Communion in Significant Autobiographical Scenes. *Journal of Personality*, *64*(2), 339–377.

Neimeyer, R. A. (2006). Re-storying loss: Fostering growth in the posttraumatic narrative. In L. G. Calhoun & R. G. Tedeschi (Eds.), *Handbook of posttraumatic growth: Research and practice* (pp. 68–80). Lawrence Erlbaum Associates.

Plaisance, P. L. (2014). *Virtue in media: The moral psychology of excellence in news and public relations*. Routledge.

Stewart, M., Reid, G., & Mangham, C. (1997). Fostering children's resilience. *Journal of Pediatric Nursing*, *12*(1), 21–31.

Vardeman, C., & Schauster, E. (2021). Familial experiences of exemplars in marketing communication. *Journal of Media Ethics*, *36*(4), 202–219.

7 Ethical Leadership

Introduction

As the Fellows shared their life stories and lessons gleaned from crucible experiences, they recalled examples of times when they demonstrated moral courage and ethical leadership and times when they wished they would have spoken up when faced with ethical dilemmas. Ethical leadership is central to public relations as it aligns with the role of issues management (Lee et al., 2006), with the objective of crisis prevention and "serving as an early warning system for potential . . . threats" (Wartick & Rude, 1986, p. 124). Public relations practitioners have described their ethics counseling responsibilities as

> encouraging companies and organizations to practice truthful and authentic communication, "pointing out what is right and what is wrong," being "unafraid to raise these questions," representing the concerns of key stakeholders, and informing "senior management . . . as to the potential ethical impact of their decisions."
>
> (Neill & Barnes, 2018, p. 11)

One common thread in the Fellows' experiences is that several of them had attended Catholic schools or universities and credit their Jesuit education as their ethical and moral foundation. As Bob Frause explained:

> You take five courses in philosophy; you take three courses in theology as part of the liberal arts curriculum. You take an ethics – well, I took two ethics classes, one a philosophical ethics class, one in ethics in journalism – I mean, you just get a really solid education and essentially a moral beacon.

This foundation proved essential for Michelle Egan, who has made ethics a central focus in her role as national chair of PRSA for 2023. She has

DOI: 10.4324/9781003451709-7

faced several ethical dilemmas in her career, none more challenging than one involving a family member. She had suspicions that they had committed a crime. She explained what happened next:

> I spoke to an attorney about my suspicions. And I shared that I wasn't really certain, but I suspected something very wrong was happening. And she said, 'I don't really know you. I've only just met you. But you do not seem like the kind of person who could keep that to yourself. So, if you would like to go meet with the police and provide this information, I will go with you.'

The police asked Egan to wear a wire in order to have evidence to prosecute the case. She sought counsel from a Jesuit priest who said, "Well, one of the things that we do in discernment is we ask, where would the greatest good be done?" Egan described the dilemma she faced:

> I kept asking myself, how are you going to explain to your family why you did this? And what pushed me over the edge was the question that came to my mind, which is how would you explain why you didn't? And so, I took the actions that I needed to take. It was very difficult – they were arrested and spent time in jail.

This type of moral reasoning is often referred to as *consequentialism*, which requires decision makers to consider the potential consequences of their actions to determine whether they are being ethical (Lemoine et al., 2019). Other moral reasoning approaches include deontology, which involves examining "the act itself and whether it is judged as correct according to set standards of behavior," and virtue ethics, which suggests "true morality arises from the reflection and consideration of the wise and the self-aware" (Lemoine et al., 2019, pp. 165, 168; Anscombe, 1958). It appears that virtue ethics was a consideration of Egan because she also reflected on how the action would be consistent with her personal values and character. Moral courage such as Egan demonstrated requires the "fortitude to convert moral intentions into actions despite pressures from either inside or outside of the organization to do otherwise" (May et al., 2003, p. 255). It requires moral efficacy or "confidence in one's abilities" in order to "justify a courageous moral action" and willingness to deal with potential opposition (May et al., 2014, p. 71; May et al., 2003). Based on qualitative and survey research with practitioners, Neill (2021, 2023) has identified ten essential ethics competencies or abilities that are necessary in public relations: (1) Personal code of conduct/Ethics/ Values system, (2) Personal behavior/Integrity/Accountability/Trustworthiness, (3) Awareness/Knowledge of code of ethics/Identify ethical issues/Discernment, (4) Critical thinking/ Problem solving, (5) Honesty/Transparency/

Truthfulness/Candor, (6) Courage/Speak truth to power, (7) Strategic Planning, (8) Judgment, (9) Counseling abilities/Ability to articulate and provide recommendations/Oral Communication, and (10) Leadership/Team building. One of the competencies found to be most lacking in our profession is courage (Neill, 2021, 2023). A recent study also revealed that those who had completed accreditation or certification programs, which include formal training and testing focused specifically on ethics and law, such as the APR (Accreditation in Public Relations), had more confidence in their ethics competencies and also more frequently engaged in ethics counseling (Neill, 2023).

As mentioned previously, several of the Fellows received ethics training specifically through Catholic schools and universities, as well as their parents, churches, and the APR program. As Michelle Egan explained:

> There were some moments that really solidified my commitment to this particular career. Probably the peak moment was going through the accreditation process and particularly learning about and applying the code of ethics in the way that is expected. It really brought everything together for me. It brought together the sort of values that my family had, the experiences I had in college at a Jesuit university and the focus on ethics and social justice. Studying for the APR made clear the importance of this role, its impact on society and how it connects to my personal values.

As another example of moral courage, Bob Frause recounted the time he chased down a bank robber in the mid-1980s:

> I was going to lunch, I had a coat and tie on, a raincoat, dress shoes, and walking down the street of Seattle, and all of a sudden, somebody yells, "Get that man, he just robbed the bank!" And so, I thought to myself – I was running 30 miles a week or so, so I was in pretty good shape . . . But essentially, I said to myself, "I can catch that guy," and so I turned around and started running after him. And I ran down the street and I told him, I said, "You can run all you want, but I'm going to catch you." And I didn't know if he had a gun or whatever – he had this big money bag. So, then we ran across the street, up another block, and I finally caught him in a doorway and I turned him around and I said, "Give me that bag," and I grabbed the bag out of his hand and then I started back to the bank. Well, it turns out there was $100,000 in the bag. I guess I walked all the way back and then the cops were already there. I gave them the bag, and then they wanted me to get in the cop car to see if they could find the guy, and we found him two blocks around another corner.

This example is consistent with previous findings on moral exemplars as "people who translate their principles into action directly, with little indecision or hesitation" (Colby & Damon, 1992, p. 70). Frause explained his actions by describing his core values:

> Looking away is probably the worst thing that a human being can do – is be somewhere and then decide that, you know, I'm not involved, and it's not my problem and I'm going to look away, because it is your problem. That's what that bank robbery thing was that I explained to you earlier. Looking away is horrendous. People are out there and they deserve – if they need help – they deserve to be helped.

Note his focus on helping people in need, which is consistent with the *communion* theme of *care/help* (McAdams et al., 1996). Frause would later serve on the PRSA Board of Ethics and Professional Standards and lead a multiyear effort to revise the code of ethics in 2000.

Renea Morris described a time when her husband showed moral courage. They were youth ministers and lived in Los Angeles in 1992 when the Rodney King riots broke out following the acquittal of the police officers involved in the beating:

> I remember watching TV when the riots started. We did not live too far away from the epicenter, so I could actually hear what was going on around me. I called him because I figured he didn't know what was going on because he was working downtown. And I told him, I said, "You need to avoid Florence and Normandie when you come home." My husband is a very caring person. That's exactly where he went. He was considered one of the heroes of the riots because he saved several motorists during that time. I figured he was there because it was like two hours later when he came home. He had blood all over his shirt. I didn't know if he had been shot or what had happened. It turned out that it was somebody else's blood.

Her husband was honored by the city for his heroic efforts that day. In response, she and her husband demonstrated ethical leadership by creating a nonprofit organization called the Youth Job Awareness Project to address some of the root issues of the unrest, including high employment and poverty. They set up a hotline for people looking for jobs and hosted a job fair. As Morris explained:

> And the job fair motto was that everybody who came to the job fair would get an interview. They would sit at roundtables with actual hiring managers and find out what it would take to get the job. We had typewriters at that time to do resumes. We fed them, and several people got jobs right from their interview on the spot. So, when I tell you that this was like the best of times and the worst of times, it was because obviously, you know, there was a lot more need than what we could actually support.

As a result of their efforts, Governor Pete Wilson established the California Commission for Improving Life Through Service, and its legacy continues 30 years later. This work is core to Morris' personal mission. As she expressed, "I feel my job is to help people figure out what their why is."

This narrative again demonstrates *communion* themes of *care/help* and *community*, which represents the "idea of being part of a larger community, experiencing a sense of oneness, unity, harmony, synchrony, togetherness, belongingness, allegiance, or solidarity with a group of people, a community, or even all of humankind together" (McAdams et al., 1996, p. 351). Both of the examples provided by Frause and Morris are consistent with *ethics of care*, a moral philosophy which emphasizes that the self and others are interdependent (Gilligan, 1982) and that "detachment, whether from self or from others, is morally problematic, since it breeds moral blindness or indifference – a failure to discern or respond to need" (Gilligan, 1987, p. 24). Fisher and Tronto (1990) identified four steps associated with caring: (1) caring about (i.e., recognizing needs), (2) taking care of (i.e., assuming responsibility for caring), (3) caregiving (i.e., hands-on work), and (4) care-receiving (e.g., response by the one receiving care). The example discussed by Morris demonstrated these steps in actual practice.

On the other extreme, Ron Culp did not report an incident that made him uncomfortable regarding expense reporting:

> Early in my corporate career, I was asked to speak at training programs for prospective salespeople about the role of PR in order to enlist them as a first line of insight when they heard things that should be on our radar. At the end of one day of training, I joined the trainees for drinks. As we were preparing to leave, each of us pitched in our portion of the check when one of the salesmen reached over and takes the now-paid check, which was well over $100, only a few dollars of which were for his beers. He said, "This is as good as gold." Moral dilemma – I am a manager who hadn't yet gone through the company's extensive training program but I knew this was wrong. However, as a fairly new manager, I simply made a mental note and put the incident in the back of my mind.

Fast forward a few years and Culp is asked to consider this same man for a job:

> Little did I ever expect that the head of HR would ask me to interview this guy, and when I said no, he said, "You have to." And then the pressure came and the EVP, who I reported to, told me I had to do the interview, and I again said, "No, I can't." They demanded to know why, and I told them about the bar bill observation. As it turned out, this young person was a friend of a very senior member of the company who wanted to help advance his career. At that moment, I realized my career might be affected,

but I held firm. One of these senior leaders told me to, "Get over it, kid. Interview the guy." Morally, I realized I had to take a stand since I could never trust the guy. He eventually landed in a position elsewhere in the company. Today, most organizations clearly spell out ethical guidelines and requirements that would cover such observations, even if the incident doesn't happen in your area of responsibility.

As a result of this experience, Culp closely scrutinized expense reports throughout his career and became a stickler for ethical conduct.

Mark Dvorak recalled two specific experiences: one when he raised an ethical issue and one when he wished he would have spoken up. The first scenario involved counseling a client regarding social media:

> Social media was in its infancy, particularly for businesses. Which meant we were all still operating without generally accepted ethical practices. In one meeting with a client, we were discussing likes and reposts and all the new terminology. My client was not at all appreciating what some folks online were saying about the products she represented. And she essentially said, "Why don't you all go create accounts and go on and refute what they are posting." As I said earlier, about how ethics have always been "common sense" to me, there was no lack of clarity in my brain. I had to be very diplomatic in what I said – and the specific language is gone from my memory now – but I said, "No." Looking back, it was the first time I think I truly lived up to the role of counselor – painting a picture for her long-term implications. I made it clear I thought her idea was not only wrong, but the eventual consequences also would be painful. That moved her.

The second scenario involved being asked to pitch to a potential client working in the payday lending sector. Dvorak explained his discomfort at the time:

> As an office, we weren't in a strong financial position when the opportunity presented itself. And I was new to the agency, so I didn't feel like I could raise concerns. Today it's a different story altogether. We have very clear guidelines about industries we'll not even entertain the idea of working for. And if you personally object to a company or organization we do choose to work with, you can opt out. No harm, no foul. But back when this pitch was coming together, I think I had just been at the agency a month or two. So, I was more nervous than usual presenting with a new boss and colleagues. I'm also learning how this pitching thing works in the agency world. Throughout the presentation and for the following weeks until we learned we weren't selected I just kept praying. "No, no, we can't win this. We can't win this." And I think if we had won it and if I had to work on it, I would have left.

He said battling cancer has changed his perspective:

> That really changed me and very much made me more cognizant of what I was doing and where I was headed, and what is important to me. The payday lending pitch happened a year or two before my cancer. I'd like to believe I would have spoken up at the time and said, "No, I don't want to do it." But I can't say that with certainty. Maybe I would have just done it. Today, there is not a chance in a million I would put pay over principle. I would go back to bagging groceries at Publix like I did at 16 before I do anything that preys on people.

Demonstrating Ethical Leadership

These examples demonstrate that public relations practitioners develop as ethical leaders and counselors as they face "trial by fire" experiences or crucibles (Place, 2019). Ethical leadership requires being both a moral or ethical person and a moral manager (Treviño et al., 2000). "Being viewed as an ethical person means that people think of you as having certain traits [e.g., honesty, trustworthiness, and integrity], engaging in certain kinds of behaviors, and making decisions based upon ethical principles" (Treviño et al., 2000, p. 130). Moral managers need to serve as a role model based on their personal conduct, routinely communicate about the importance of ethical standards and values, and use reward systems to encourage ethical behavior (Treviño et al., 2000). Michelle Egan demonstrated that ethical leadership when she provided counsel to the company president following a crisis. A contractor employee was in an accident that resulted in the death of a middle school boy who was riding his bicycle home from school. She described the moral dilemma:

> Over a couple of days, an exchange occurred between the members of the executive team about what kind of engagement the president should have. This was not a public relations issue; it was a private matter. The president, a retired military leader asked me, "Do you think I should call his mother?" Some counseled against it; we didn't yet know all of the facts. The president and I had a conversation about it and I said, "Look, this is who you are. You reach out to people when they're hurting. You've been in many situations where you had to go tell someone's wife that her pilot husband is not coming home. Is this what you think you want to do?" And he responded, "Well, that's what I would normally do, but I understand if we shouldn't." And the execs really debated it back and forth, raising lots of important issues. In the end, he made the call and it was a very sad day, but he did what was most aligned with his values, which happened to be aligned with the company's values.

The Fellows understood and embraced their role as an ethics counselor, which involves "a lack of impulsiveness, care in mapping out alternatives and consequences . . . and awareness of and concern for the effects of one's decision and policies on others" (Goodpaster & Matthews, 1982, p. 134). Olga Mayoral Wilson provided ethics counsel to the chairman of a bank following a federal investigation into a money laundering case. She demonstrated moral courage by encouraging him to be transparent with the media and the people of Puerto Rico:

> The bank's president and CEO was in his office holding yet another informal meeting with the corporation attorneys, the Washington, D.C. law firm attorneys, the New York law firm attorneys, and the company's loyal senior leadership. You get the picture. Then, I'm called to join in and we're all there. He starts talking . . . because that's his style – he speaks and shares. And then, follows with a period of silence to think, to internalize, and to analyze. He turned around, and asked me, "What would you do? What do you recommend?" At that point, the general leadership and internal consensus was for the CEO not to face the media at all, no interviews on TV nor any media – local or statewide. "It will all go away with time," was the belief shared with the Chair. Or "this will go on; nobody will notice, you know." I knew then that what I was going to say, to answer was against everybody's belief. And, I answered,
>
>> Well, I think that they – meaning your customers, your employees, your community, the media, the public who follow the Bank's over 100-year traditions and innovative services and products, they all need to see you, see your eyes. They need to hear your voice. And they need to see your face. You have to tell them this story and you tell them with your heart, which is going to be easy for you because you're hurting. You are going to explain what you can explain. But you also have to share what you cannot share.

When asked what gave her the courage to speak up that day, Mayoral Wilson explained it was consistent with her character and professional reputation:

> I think that at some point earlier, in one of the many one-on-one interviews conducted, he [the bank chairman] asked a question. And I answered, "Well, I will tell you always what my professional assessment is. It may not be what you want to hear, but you will get that from me, my opinion based on an ethical assessment."

Rebecca Villarreal demonstrated wisdom in handling an ethical dilemma while working for an education foundation. There had been some disputes with volunteers that involved being good stewards of their finances. She explained her response:

> I decided to put together a subcommittee to create financial guidelines for this new foundation. Three of us met. We created the guidelines. We presented them to the whole board, and they were adopted. So, flash forward a couple of months after the adoption, I now had something to crutch onto and say, "No, we can't do that because our guidelines say this. I didn't create these guidelines. This committee and the board created these guidelines."

Margaret Ann Hennen stood firm when asked to do something unethical by a colleague from another nation. As she explained:

> We'd worked together on a number of projects, and he wanted me to do something which in his country was completely okay. But in our country was not. It was a *pay for play* kind of thing; he wanted me to write this letter. I was taken aback by it. And I think I must have talked to him on the phone when he asked me that. Then I walked over to his office because I was big on walking over to people's offices instead of picking up the telephone because I think the face to face is important. And I said, "I can't do this." "What do you mean you can't do this?" I said, "I have a code of ethics in my profession. And this would be against my code of ethics." He said, "You have a code of ethics?" This was foreign to him. We talked for a long time. And I said, "I can't do what you're asking. but I can do this." And he said okay.

Hennen resolved the issue by engaging in dialogue and offering an ethical alternative. She added:

> It wasn't that he was unethical. It was just I don't think anybody had ever explained to him that in our country he was asking for something that we considered unethical. Because in his own country, it was not. But that code of ethics of PRSA has been my guiding principle for a long time.

Philip Tate also drew from the PRSA code of ethics when counseling a colleague who was facing an ethical dilemma:

> I recently offered some counsel to a PR agency friend, who was dealing with a situation with a client, who was asking my friend to leak something to the media, and he was really conflicted about it. I told him, "Trust your gut. If it doesn't feel right to you, it probably isn't." I suggested that he refer to the PRSA Code of Ethics. The situation he outlined dealt with

issues like disclosure of information and safeguarding confidences. The client had asked my friend, "Here's some information that I have. I want you to give this to someone you know in the media, so that this gets out there." The client was not being fully transparent about what they were trying to do. Again, my counsel to my friend was,

> What do you know about the reliability of the information that your client is giving to you? Is it truthful? Is it accurate? Would you have a chance to fact check the information or are you just passing along bad information to the media? And most importantly, what could this do to your reputation?

When Counsel Is Not Respected and Followed

Sometimes ethics counsel can fall on deaf ears, which can be discouraging. When this happens, public relations leaders essentially have three choices: "(1) drop the issue and recognize the reality that they are not the final decision maker, (2) raise the concern to someone else, or (3) remove themselves from the situation by looking for another job or resigning" (Neill & Barnes, 2018, p. 67). Egan described that difficult season and how she responded:

> I have been so fortunate to be able to work with leaders who are really grounded, who know who they are, who are positive and care about people… But a few years ago, I was working for a leader who wasn't that way. And many of the things that I – you know issues I would raise, concerns that I would raise about the way things were going were dismissed. And they were things that I felt were really integral to the character of our company and who we are. And that was a very challenging time. And I have a little sort of saying, I guess because in our jobs, a lot of times we're like out there saying, like, are you sure you want to do that? Hey, have you thought about this? I'm not sure that's the right thing. You know, is that consistent with our values? Sometimes you say those things so many times and you're not getting any traction and it is hard. And so, what I say to myself is sometimes you just have to go underground for a little while and get your – catch your breath, right. Not that I wouldn't speak up if something was going terribly wrong, but I did have that experience over about a two-year period, and it was very, very difficult. It was draining and challenging and I wasn't underground the entire time, but you know, I learned a lot from that, too, about taking care of myself.

The way Egan handled this issue demonstrates that public relations practitioners likely consider factors associated with *moral intensity* when deciding how firm of a stance to take in regard to a particular issue (Jones, 1991). Jones (1991) provided six factors associated with moral intensity: (1) the *magnitude of the consequences*, which focuses on the potential harms or benefits of the act; (2) *social consensus* or the degree of social agreement that a proposed act is evil or good; (3) *probability of effect*, which refers to both the likelihood that the act will take place and that harm or benefit will result; (4) *time*, meaning when there is less time pressure, there is also less urgency; (5) *proximity*, refers to how close we feel to the victims or beneficiaries (i.e., stakeholders) associated with the act; and 6) *concentration of effect*, refers to the number of people affected by the action.

Michael McDougall confronted an ethical dilemma that involved a colleague publicly sharing false information to the media following a natural disaster overseas, which he considered worthy of raising within his organization or high in *moral intensity*:

> I was traveling and asleep when it happened, and when I woke, a peer in my office said,
>
>> Well, you were asleep. So, I told the team to say we were activating our employee assistance program throughout the region. I know we don't have such a program, but nobody else is going to know that. It's going to look great from a media perspective.
>
> This colleague was setting us up for failure. I went to the mat on that, and ultimately lost with the CEO. He said, "It's done. Keep your mouth shut. We have to move on." That was the start of me thinking this is no longer the organization for me.

McDougall said he responded by encouraging the company to set up an actual fund for those in need, but he eventually chose to leave the organization several months later. He described the difficulty that executives face when choosing whether or not to address ethical dilemmas, akin to "golden handcuffs" (Berger, 2005):

> You're handcuffed by your compensation structure. You're handcuffed by where you are in life. Some people feel handcuffed by family and you have to account for those factors. But at some point, you also want to be happy and/or do your best work. Then it's time to move on.

McDougall explained how this stance was core to his character and beliefs:

> For me, I think there's a sense of being honest, being truthful, not being disingenuous, which in this profession can sometimes be tough, but those instincts are also a good guide. I was in one role where I stopped believing what I was saying on behalf of an organization. That was a signal to exit. But first, let's see if we can correct it. Let's see if we can shift the mindset.

That wasn't where the organization wanted to go. If I can't believe it and I don't see enough truth in it, I'm not going to be the mouthpiece for it.

Fellows Core Values and Virtues

To better understand their ethical perspectives, the life story interviews included in-depth discussions with the Fellows regarding their core values and personal virtues. Wines and Hamilton (2009) described values as "strongly held qualities, virtues, or personal characteristics that we admire, defend, and in which we are willing to invest ourselves" (p. 438). Gert (1998) described a moral virtue as "any character trait that involves justifiably obeying the moral rules or justifiably following the moral ideals"; and a moral vice is "any character trait that involves unjustifiably violating the moral rules or that involves failing to follow the moral ideals when this can be done justifiably" (p. 285). Virtues that previously have been associated with serving as an ethical counselor or conscience in public relations include humility, truth/honesty, integrity, moral courage, caring, empathy, and candor (Neill, 2021). Consistent with these previous findings, some of the specific values and virtues that Fellows esteemed included compassion, fairness, integrity/honesty, and justice. Blake Lewis described his values, which are tied to his personal faith:

> I think that grace and forgiveness and mercy are generic terms – they certainly have a place in many – if not all – of organized faith and spirituality. But if one chooses not to pursue that, I think those three words still work pretty well. And I have to rebuke myself – one of my favorite terms – with reasonable frequency to ask if I'm demonstrating grace and forgiveness, patience, mercy to people. [It] doesn't matter what they've done to me, because I'm sure that the worst things that have been done to me are probably pretty junior varsity compared to the worst things I've probably done to other people at some point in my life.

Consistent with this perspective, based on a personality inventory of PRSA Fellows assessed through survey research, Plaisance et al. (2023) found they scored high on the Agreeableness trait, which is associated with forgiveness, gentleness, flexibility, and patience (Lee & Ashton, 2004). Other dominant personality characteristics of the Fellows were Conscientiousness, which is associated with organization, diligence, perfectionism, and prudence; and Honesty/Humility, which includes the dimensions of sincerity, fairness, modesty, and avoidance of greed (Plaisance et al., 2023; Lee & Ashton, 2004).

Col. Christian Patterson listed his personal virtue as caring. He described an example that demonstrated his care for others. He had a soldier on his team that wanted to be a military broadcast journalist, but his voice quality held him back. He provided counsel to him:

> I told him, "Look, I'm going to have a little program with you, called Chris' eggs." So, I bought a dozen eggs and I had some sharpies, and I took Tim and the entire staff in our breakroom one day, and I wrote all these things on the eggs. And I told Sergeant Morgan, I said, "If you do what I tell you to do in terms of what's written on these eggs, I guarantee you that you will be a success." And so, I wrote all these things on the eggs, and then I even made a special logo to go on the eggs. And then I said,

> > We're going to put these eggs in the refrigerator. And a year from now, if you've done these things, and it didn't work out for you in terms of success, then I'm going to take those eggs and bust them on my forehead in front of the staff.

> And everybody was just like, wow. So, a year later comes, and then it was time to do Morgan's eggs. And he did all the things and I did not have egg on my face. And the byproduct of him doing those things is that in 2016, he became the National Guard Bureau Broadcast Journalist of the Year, and now he is the senior producer for video products for Focus on the Family out in Colorado.

Col. Patterson shared the core principles and values that guide him as a leader:

> Unity, servant leadership, doing what's right, and emotional intelligence are very important. In addition, helping those who wrong you, being willing to forgive and being fair are paramount. I try to live by Philippians 2:3 which requires believers to "do nothing from rivalry or conceit, but in humility, count others more significant than yourselves." I also deeply believe in the Army values: leadership, duty, respect, selfless service, honor, integrity, and personal courage.

Mary Deming Barber values the virtues of love and kindness, which her grandmother exemplified for her:

> She always greeted you with a smile, no matter what was going on in her life. She always wanted to know what you were doing rather than telling you what she was doing. Marnie really believed that love is love. As we got older, we brought a friend over to see her. Alan [her now husband] had to meet her before we could get married. She would ask what the person did and what their interests were. And we didn't realize at first what she

was doing, but she would read up on whatever they were doing. So, here's this almost 90-year-old woman meeting my soon to be fiancé. She said, "So could you tell me how you program those computers?" Because I told her that he taught computer classes. And she thought okay, well I need to learn how to do that. She didn't have a computer. She didn't have a smartphone. But the first thing she asked him was 'how do you program those computers?' Because she was interested in what he was doing and what he cared about. She wanted to know what mattered to you.

Based on her grandmother's example, Barber summed up her core beliefs:

I believe that God teaches us and tells us to love everyone and we need to take care of each other. We need to take care of our world. And we need to work together to do that.

Philip Tate also values kindness as a virtue and considers it a personal choice:

Given the choice, I'll always choose to be kind. Being mean, being confrontational, being quick to anger – I've always viewed those actions as choices. You can certainly choose to behave that way. Or you can choose another approach by being kind to other people. Being kind is also a choice and if someone perceives me as being weak, or somehow less for being kind, fine, I'll accept that criticism. But I'd rather have people look back at their interactions with me, and say he was fair, he was kind, and he was always looking for what would be best for all parties in that situation.

Consistent with virtue ethics, Neill (2021) provided a list of questions for public relations professionals to consider when addressing ethical issues:

1) What would an ethical counselor/conscience do in this situation?
2) What are the concerns of stakeholders in this situation and have I shared those concerns with senior leaders?
3) What are some potential moral consequences of this decision?
4) Who should I consult for advice in this situation?
5) Is this decision consistent with my character and values? (p. 63)

Public relations professionals should consider these questions and what virtues are consistent with their core beliefs and values.

Questions to Consider

1. Which ethics competencies do you believe you have mastered and which ones do you need to improve?

2. What are the core ethics principles and values that guide your decision making?
3. How can you demonstrate ethical leadership in your company or organization?

References

Anscombe, G. E. M. (1958). Modern moral philosophy. *Philosophy*, *33*(124), 1–19.

Berger, B. K. (2005). Power over, power with, and power to relations: Critical reflections on public relations, the dominant coalition, and activism. *Journal of Public Relations Research*, *17*(1), 5–28. http://dx.doi.org/10.1207/s1532754xjprr1701_3

Colby, A., & Damon, W. (1992). *Some do care: Contemporary lives of moral commitment*. New York: MacMillan, Inc.

Fisher, B., & Tronto, J. (1990). Toward a feminist theory of caring. In E. K. Abel & M. K. Nelson (Eds.), *Circles of care: Work and identity in women's lives* (pp. 35–62). State University of New York Press.

Gert, B. (1998). *Morality: Its nature and justification*. Oxford University Press.

Gilligan, C. (1982). *In a different voice: Psychological theory and women's development*. Harvard University Press.

Gilligan, C. (1987). Moral orientation and moral development. In E. Kittay & D. Meyers (Eds.), *Women and moral theory* (pp. 19–33). Rowman and Littlefield Publishers.

Goodpaster, K. E., & Matthews, J. B. (1982). Can a corporation have a conscience? *Harvard Business Review*, *60*(1), 132–141.

Jones, T. M. (1991). Ethical decision making by individuals in organizations: An issue-contingent model. *Academy of Management Review*, *16*(2), 366–395.

Lee, J., Heath, R., & Bowen, S. (2006). *An international study of ethical roles and counsel in the public relations function* [Paper presentation]. Conference Papers, International Communication Association, pp. 1–37, Dresden, Germany.

Lee, K., & Ashton, M. C. (2004). Psychometric properties of the HEXACO personality inventory. *Multivariate Behavioral Research*, *39*(2), 329–358. https://doi.org/10.1207/s15327906mbr3902_8

Lemoine, G. J., Hartnell, C. A., & Leroy, H. (2019). Taking stock of moral approaches to leadership: An integrative review of ethical, authentic, and servant leadership. *Academy of Management Journal*, *13*(1), 148–187.

May, D. R., Chan, A. Y. L., Hodges, T. D., & Avolio, B. J. (2003). Developing the moral component of authentic leadership. *Organizational Dynamics*, *32*(3), 247–260.

May, D. R., Luth, M. T., & Schwoerer, C. E. (2014). The influence of business ethics education on moral efficacy, moral meaningfulness, and moral courage: A quasi-experimental study. *Journal of Business Ethics*, *124*, 67–80.

McAdams, D. P., Hoffman, B. J., Mansfield, E. D., & Day, R. (1996). Themes of agency and communion in significant autobiographical scenes. *Journal of Personality*, *64*(2), 339–377.

Neill, M. S. (2021). Public relations professionals identify ethical issues, essential competencies & deficiencies. *Journal of Media Ethics*, *36*(1), 51–67. https://doi.org/10.1080/23736992.2020.1846539

Neill, M. S. (2023). The state of ethics competencies, training & moral efficacy in public relations. *Journal of Media Ethics*. https://doi.org/10.1080/23736992.2023.2228305

Neill, M. S., & Barnes, A. (2018). *Public relations ethics: Senior PR pros tell us how to speak up and keep your job.* Business Expert Press.

Place, K. R. (2019). Moral dilemmas, trials, and gray areas: Exploring on-the-job moral development of public relations professionals. *Public Relations Review, 45,* 24–34.

Plaisance, P. L., Neill, M., & Chen, J. (2023). Moral orientations and traits of public relations exemplars. *Journal of Public Relations Research.* https://doi.org/10.1080/1062726X.2023.2250034

Treviño, L. K., Hartman, L. P., & Brown, M. (2000). Moral person and moral manager: How executives develop a reputation for ethical leadership. *California Management Review, 42*(4), 128–142.

Wartick, S. L., & Rude, R. E. (1986). Issues management: Corporate fad or corporate function? *California Management Review, 29*(1), 124–140.

Wines, W. A., & Hamilton, J. B., III. (2009). On changing organizational cultures by injecting new ideologies: The power of stories. *Journal of Business Ethics, 89,* 433–447.

8 Conclusion
The Future of Ethical Leadership

Introduction

The personal stories shared in this book demonstrate the importance of the PRSA College of Fellows and their commitment to "sharing what we have learned, striving to inspire others, and being role models to professionals and students of our craft and to those communities we serve" (PRSA College of Fellows Values, n.d.). Consistent with previous research, as the Fellows discussed the next phase of their lives, "themes of caring for the next generation, of leaving a positive legacy for the future, of giving something back to society for the benefits one has received, and other generative motifs become increasingly salient in life stories" (McAdams, 2001, p. 107; McAdams et al., 1993).

Future Chapters and Life Projects

Giving back and sharing wisdom were common themes as the Fellows discussed the next chapter of their lives, as their plans involved activities such as teaching, mentoring, writing books, or volunteer service. Blake Lewis explained his motivation:

> My responsibility is to hand that wisdom off to other people who are in different places than me, either age wise, experience wise, setting or climate wise, and make sure that I've not squandered that on just myself, because some of the greatest things that I've been able to accomplish were because there were caring people, some of whom had no reason, right, or motivation, necessarily, to do so, but gifted me experiences and quips and things that informed and guided me in my path.

Lewis has become involved in a range of activities that allow community organizations to benefit from his extensive expertise, such as chairing the board of a nonprofit in North Texas that focuses on reducing and eliminating barriers to education for youth that are at risk, and serving as a public safety volunteer and crisis response volunteer for the Office of Emergency Management in several cities in the Dallas-Fort Worth area.

DOI: 10.4324/9781003451709-8

Commander Christian Patterson discussed his efforts to "pay it forward":

> I'm a member of the Alpha Phi Alpha Fraternity, Inc. alumni chapter in Canton, Mississippi, which is about 13 miles north of Jackson. A portion of our service area includes Holmes County, which is one of the poorest counties in the entire country. Our chapter is committed to helping them as much as possible. During the elections season, we execute a special voter registration and education initiative for them. In the past, I've printed and emplaced hundreds of door hangers in the Tchula and Lexington communities to remind their residents to vote and help them understand their rights with the process. I'm really passionate about connecting with people and helping them to thrive in every area of life.

Mary Deming Barber has been serving on the city council in her community. She shared a blog post that she wrote regarding her core beliefs:

> I do this because I believe that each one of us can make a difference. I believe in man's desire to do good and make the world a better place. That's not to say I don't ever get discouraged or anxious. Leaders are human, after all. But leaders focus on doing good, on what can be done alone but also on what can be accomplished together.[1]

Several of the Fellows expressed a desire to write books or invest in the lives of students. Judy Phair plans to continue her service with the Commission on Public Relations Education and the accrediting body, the Accrediting Council on Education in Journalism and Mass Communications (ACEJMC). As she explained:

> I'm very concerned about upholding the ethical and excellent practice of public relations long term. For example, some advances in technology are making it easier to bypass ethical checkpoints and safeguards. Being a strong, active advocate for ethics in our profession is critical.

Dr. Bey-Ling Sha reflected on her current role in higher education administration and how it fits with her values:

> I think my life project is to help other people see the bigger picture . . . Whether it's in the classroom, helping my students see the bigger picture of public relations practice as being building and maintaining relationships between organizations and organizational stakeholders, and not just

---

1 Barber, M. *This I believe.* https://magazine.thestriveproject.com/issue/oct-dec-2021/this-i-believe/

publicity or media relations . . . Maybe now it's also to help anyone working at a university see it as not just a job, especially our professors . . . It's
not just about doing your research and teaching your class and having tenure. It's about how we need to be doing this work in service to the public,
in service to the greater good, in service to democratic society . . . I feel
passionate in terms of bringing my scholarly expertise, my public relations
acumen into more conspicuous play in service to a really big, important
mission. And for the College that I lead as Dean, the mission is to pre-
pare communicators to advance democracy. But really that mission for the
country at large is to preserve and protect and advance democracy, which
is the foundation of our country.

In a similar vein, Gene Hall discussed how he has written editorial columns and social media posts to advocate for truth and agricultural issues:

> In the public square, I've kind of have a passion for truth. And in the lim-
> ited channels of communication that are open to me now, I would like to
> advocate for that. There are people that say we live in a fact free world
> now. That the facts don't matter. Well, I maintain that they do, and to the
> extent that I can, I want to point people back toward the facts. And unfor-
> tunately, some people view that as taking a political stand. And I suppose it
> is to a certain extent. But, you know, facts matter, and we can't – we can't
> build our country moving forward on lies. And so, the extent that I can,
> I want to be involved in that.

Olga Mayoral Wilson and Ana Toro plan to continue their service with
DE&I committees within PRSA. Consistent with this passion, Toro also
would like to visit colleges and universities to discuss career opportunities in
public relations:

> I feel that I am one of those faces that needs to be out there, so students
> are inspired. And especially young Latina girls and young Latino boys that
> may be saying, "But where are my leaders? Where are the people I want
> to be like them?" And that project is close to my heart, and I want to do it
> at some point in my life.

Mark McClennan plans to continue to produce his podcast "Ethical
Voices" through which he discusses ethical challenges and current issues with
public relations professionals:

> One question I ask everybody I interview for "Ethical Voices" is what is
> the best piece of ethics advice you ever received? There are some amaz-
> ing responses. The most common are the New York Times test and what

would your mother think if she read in the paper. Some other great answers were Michael Smart sharing PR pros need to always have a freedom fund. Another great response was from Helio Fred Garcia "There will come a point where you reach that ethical line. I can't predict when it will be. But I can predict that you will face that line. The question is are you looking at it in the rear-view mirror or are you looking at it through the windshield? Are you approaching the line, or have you already crossed it and now you regret it?"

There's lots of good tidbits of advice you can use all the time. Ethics advice comes from everybody. It's not based on a title. It could be the CEO, your friend next door or the people that work for you. You must keep your mind open and constantly learning. If you're not learning something new every day, you're falling behind.

Ron Culp plans to continue to maintain his blog, Culpwrit, which is focused on public relations careers:

> Because of the more than 15,000 regular readers of the Culpwrit blog, I feel compelled to date every post since it puts pressure on me for regular updates. In the early days through 10 years of blogging I wrote a blog post every week, and over the past four years I've increasingly relied on more guest posts from students and professionals who share their insights and career advice. I still try to write an original post every second or third week. Dating the posts becomes motivational. Actually, I wish all bloggers dated their posts. Doing so keeps mental pressure on to post more often. So, part of my life goal in the 'what's next' is to maintain a regular schedule of posting.

Marisa Vallbona is creating inspirational short videos and short stories:

> And I would start posting them to Instagram, Facebook and YouTube, and get really positive feedback from them. Sometimes when I wouldn't post them for a while, people would ask, "When are you going to post another video? We miss your videos." I do it because I want my sons to have inspiration and wisdom once I'm gone. My older son often calls me for advice. He ends the call jokingly saying, "I'm glad you're not dead yet." We both laugh about it, but we know our time here is limited. That's my inspiration to leave behind a legacy that no money can buy. And I think about when I'm gone, mostly because my dad left such an impressive legacy and inspired me to do the same for my sons. I want them to have a good heart and ethics. I want them to have strong faith and good values.

Consistent with this sentiment, virtue ethics stresses the importance of ethical role models "who teach us all what it is to be moral by example, not by precept. Their lives inspire us to live better lives, to be better people" (Pojman, 2005, pp. 163, 166). As previously mentioned, the Fellows are not without personal faults, but they have been recognized by their peers as exemplars who have demonstrated a commitment to the ethical practice of public relations. By examining the crucible experiences they have faced, it becomes clear how these trials develop character and virtues and equip them to be ethical leaders in their organizations and the public relations profession. The *phronesis* or practical wisdom that is necessary to provide ethical leadership can best be developed through life experiences such as crucibles (Hursthouse, 1999; Place, 2019).

What We've Learned

Here are some insights about the development of ethical leaders that can be gleaned from this study:

1. Parents and educators play a crucial role in teaching and modeling ethical behavior and values. It was encouraging that even Fellows who were raised by legal guardians rather than their parents and/or grew up in poverty thrived and referenced their early childhood experiences as foundational to the development of values.
2. Early experiences in organizations such as the Boy Scouts, Girl Scouts, FFA, or ROTC can help young adults develop leadership skills. These experiences also can develop their sense of community and desire to help others in need.
3. Some crucible experiences can be related to cultural identity, such as microaggressions and discrimination. All leaders need to develop cultural literacy and find ways to be supportive and inclusive of individuals from diverse racial, ethnic, and cultural backgrounds.
4. Everyone will face a range of different crucibles in their lifetime (e.g., new territory, reversals, or suspension), but it's how they respond to these challenges that determines whether or not lessons are learned and character is developed. Some people can become demoralized and falter when they face crucibles, while others emerge stronger and thrive.
5. Although it can be an uncomfortable experience, it is important to engage in critical reflection. This allows public relations professionals to consider what they are learning from their experiences, resulting in personal growth. This step also involves confronting one's personal weaknesses and determining how to overcome them. Young professionals need to be aware of barriers to effective self-reflection and ensure that they engage in healthy (*adaptive*) reflection. Some examples of self-reflection approaches include journal writing, seeking feedback from colleagues or mentors, and reading inspirational works (Berger & Erzikova, 2019).

6. An outcome of crucible experiences and critical reflection is "*phronesis* or practical wisdom – the hard-won moral expertise that comes from experience and reflection" (Borden, 2019, p. 172). Crucible experiences and the wisdom gleaned from those experiences have equipped Fellows to be ethical leaders and role models. This is not meant to suggest that younger professionals cannot demonstrate ethical courage and leadership, but that wisdom comes with age and experience.

7. The flourishing demonstrated in the lives of the Fellows was the result of the "reciprocal nature of social influence" meaning the Fellows were positively influenced by family members, friends, and colleagues, and then the Fellows in turn provided inspiration for others.

8. Ethics is core to the character of the Fellows to the point where they act on their values without hesitation. Developing ethics competencies through ethics training can provide the confidence necessary to have the moral courage to provide ethics counsel and speak truth to power.

9. While public relations professionals do have a responsibility to raise ethical concerns, their advice is not always heeded. They then have to decide whether to continue to press the issue or leave the organization.

10. While the Fellows were committed to achieving personal success, several of them also discussed their commitment to helping others and giving back to their communities. This *moral commitment* involves not only caring about others but also identifying needs and then assuming personal responsibility for meeting those needs (Fisher & Tronto, 1990).

Practical Advice for Young Professionals

So how can young professionals become ethical leaders?

1. They need to build their ethical awareness by becoming familiar with industry codes of ethics and similar guidelines within their own workplace. Neill (2023) has provided a list of resources to develop ten essential ethics competencies, including ethical awareness and the ability to identify ethical issues. Some of these same resources are provided in the 2023 Commission on Public Relations Education report (see Sidebar).

2. Next, young professionals need to identity ethical mentors who can provide guidance when they do face ethical dilemmas. It is important to find ethical mentors both inside and outside of their workplace.

3. Another important step is to regularly participate in ethics training. One common source of ethics training for the Fellows was pursuing the APR credential. Once professionals have achieved the APR, they are required to participate in continuing education including ongoing ethics training.

4. Next, it is important for young professionals to routinely work through ethics scenarios using decision models, similar to participating in crisis

communication drills. There are a variety of decision models that can be applied to scenarios, some of which are covered in the Page Center Ethics Training Modules (see Sidebar).

5. Finally, young professionals can learn about how to be an ethical leader by observing both good and bad behavior by leaders and learning from their successes and failures.

A Few Helpful Resources

Page Center Ethics Training Modules: www.pagecentertraining.psu.edu/

PRSA Board of Ethics and Professional Standards resources: www.prsa.org/about/ethics

Plank Center – Cracking the Code to Workplace Confidence: https://plankcenter.ua.edu/wp-content/uploads/2022/05/CrackingTheCode.pdf

Self-reflection study: http://plankcenter.ua.edu/resources/research/self-reflection-in-public-relations-leaders/

Mentorship Guide: http://bit.ly/MentorshipGuidePDF

APR Study Guide: https://accreditation.prsa.org/MyAPR/Content/Resources/Resources_for_Candidates.aspx

Directions for Future Research

While this study focused on members of the PRSA College of Fellows, future research could highlight members of the Arthur W. Page Society, who are also highly esteemed in the public relations industry. Their members include "chief communications officers (CCOs) at the world's leading companies, non-profits and government agencies; CEOs of the foremost public relations agencies, and distinguished educators from leading business and communications schools" (Arthur W. Page Society Membership, n.d.). In addition, similar studies on the impact of crucible experiences on leader development should be conducted in other nations to explore cultural differences, including other religions and political and socio-economic conditions. Participants in this study primarily grew up in Judeo-Christian households. Prior research focused on the impact of crucible experiences on the development of servant leaders did include participants from other religious traditions (Neill & Meng, 2022).

It would also be valuable to study crucibles and their impact on moral development in the lives of Millennials/Gen Y (born 1981–1996) and Gen Z (born 1997–2012) (Dimock, 2019). This would build on the findings of Craig and colleagues (2021), who conducted survey research with emerging adults with degrees in journalism and mass communication to examine their personality traits, virtues, moral reasoning, and ethical ideology. In particular, they found that emerging adults scored lower on character traits, such as bravery/courage, forgiveness/mercy and self-regulation (e.g., disciplined person; manages vices and bad habits; stays calm and cool under pressure; manages impulses and emotions), but scored high on traits such as curiosity, love of learning, and kindness (Craig et al., 2021).

Another topic worthy of future study is an examination of the quality of professional development training in public relations ethics and how programs align with the core ethics competencies as identified by public relations professionals (Neill, 2021, 2023).

It also should be mentioned that because this study was focused on leader development, ethical leadership, and identifying common characteristics of exemplars, significant differences among individual participants and their life experiences may have been overlooked or not as thoroughly examined. Future research could explore these differences among participants and their impact on moral development.

Conclusion

In today's society, there is a need for strong ethical leadership, and public relations professionals naturally have a role to fulfill in this area as their responsibilities involve issues and reputation management. Through their personal narratives, the Fellows have demonstrated what this looks like in actual practice. While they are not always successful in convincing others of the right action, they are unwavering in their personal commitment to the ethical practice of public relations and are willing to speak truth to power.

References

Arthur W. Page Society Membership. (n.d.). https://page.org/membership

Berger, B. K., & Erzikova, E. (2019). Self-reflection in public relations leaders: A study of its practice and value in Russia and North America. *Public Relations Journal, 13*(1), 1–22.

Borden, S. L. (2019). Virtue ethics & media. In P. L. Plaisance (Ed.), *Communication and media ethics* (pp. 171–190). Walter de Gruyter.

Commission on Public Relations Education Report. (2023). www.commissionpred.org/research/

Craig, D. A., Plaisance, P. L., Schauster, E., Thomas, R. J., Roberts, C., Place, K. R., Sun, Y., & Chen, J., Yetter, C., & Thomas, R. L. (2021). Moving into the media world: The moral psychology of emerging adults in journalism and communication. *Journalism & Mass Communication Educator, 76*(3), 314–337. https://doi.org/10.1177/1077695821992244

Dimock, M. (2019). Defining generations: Where millennials end and generation Z begins. *Pew Research Center.* www.pewresearch.org/short-reads/2019/01/17/where-millennials-end-and-generation-z-begins/

Fisher, B., & Tronto, J. (1990). Toward a feminist theory of caring. In E. K. Abel & M. K. Nelson (Eds.), *Circles of care: Work and identity in women's lives* (pp. 35–62). State University of New York Press.

Hursthouse, R. (1999). *On virtue ethics.* Oxford University Press.

McAdams, D. P. (2001). The psychology of life stories. *Review of General Psychology, 5*(2), 100–122.

McAdams, D. P., de St. Aubin, E., & Logan, R. (1993). Generativity among young, midlife, and older adults. *Psychology and Aging, 8,* 221–230.

Neill, M. S. (2021). Public relations professionals identify ethical issues, essential competencies & deficiencies. *Journal of Media Ethics, 36*(1), 51–67. https://doi.org/10.1080/23736992.2020.1846539

Neill, M. S. (2023). The state of ethics competencies, training & moral efficacy in public relations. *Journal of Media Ethics.* https://doi.org/10.1080/23736992.2023.2228305

Neill, M. S., & Meng, J. (2022). The impact of crucibles in developing public relations' character & competencies as servant leaders. *Journal of Media Ethics, 37*(3), 208–222. https://doi.org/10.1080/23736992.2022.2107526

Place, K. R. (2019). Moral dilemmas, trials, and gray areas: Exploring on-the-job moral development of public relations professionals. *Public Relations Review, 45*(1), 24–34. https://doi.org/10.1016/j.pubrev.2018.12.005

Pojman, L. P. (2005). *How should we live? An introduction to ethics.* Thomson Wadsworth.

PRSA College of Fellows Values. (n.d.). www.prsa.org/docs/default-source/about/get-involved/college-of-fellows/college-of-fellows-values.pdf?sfvrsn=f4af96b0_0

Appendix A
Biographies

J.W. Arnold, APR, Fellow PRSA

J.W. Arnold, APR, Fellow PRSA, is the 2023 chair of the PRSA College of Fellows. A successful independent practitioner for more than 24 years, he is also a leader of PRSA's indie community. He helped revitalize the Independent Practitioners Alliance section and later founded the popular IndieCHATs during the pandemic. The twice-weekly Zoom mastermind group offers participants networking and professional development opportunities, and has attracted more than 300 indies over the first three years. Arnold created the PR Consultants' Business Boot Camp, and he regularly coaches other independent practitioners. He was awarded the Pat Jackson Award for Distinguished Service to PRSA in 2022. Arnold holds degrees from Central Methodist University and the University of Auckland, New Zealand, where he studied as a Rotary Foundation scholar.

Ann H. Barkelew, Founding General Manager, FleishmanHillard, Minneapolis/St, Paul (retired)

Ann H. Barkelew's 35-year public relations career includes C-suite experience in the public sector (Los Angeles County Office of Education), the private sector (Dayton Hudson Corporation, aka Target Corporation) and with a major international agency (Fleishman Hillard). In 1995, she was named by her peers internationally as "Public Relations Professional of the Year" in *PR News*; in 1999, was named one of the Most Influential Women in Business in Minnesota by *CityBusiness*; in 2001, received Fleishman-Hillard's Lifetime Achievement Award; and in 2003, received the Arthur W. Page Society's Distinguished Service Award for contributions that have strengthened the role of public relations in society. In 2011, she received the University of Alabama's Plank Center's Legacy Award for Mentoring and in 2016 was named a Marvelous Mentor by Twin Cities Business Monthly. In 2017, Ann received the inaugural Larry Foster Award for Integrity in Public Communication from the Arthur W. Page Center at Penn State.

Barbara Burfeind, APR+M, Fellow PRSA

Barbara Burfeind, APR+M, Fellow PRSA, is an educator, communication consultant, and active mentor. She is currently an adjunct professor at George Mason University in Fairfax, Virginia, teaching Public Relations campaigns and PR writing. Burfeind is a longtime PRSA member, past president of the PRSA National Capital Chapter, and accredited in Public Relations + Military communication (APR+M). She was inducted into the PRSA College of Fellows in October 2012, recognizing her more than 20 years of contributions to the profession. She was the 2020 and 2021 PRSA National Capital Chapter APR committee co-chair and recipient of the NCC 2021 Platinum Award for outstanding service. Burfeind retired as a Navy public affairs officer in 2004 and from the federal government in 2020, working in strategic communication and visual communication. She has a bachelor's degree in communication from Syracuse University and a master's degree in communication from the University of Oklahoma.

Jeremy C. Burton, APR, Fellow PRSA

Jeremy C. Burton, APR, Fellow PRSA, is a speaker, author, and an award-winning public relations professional. Jeremy is a global leader in creating strategic communications programs for Christian nonprofits. His contagious enthusiasm and passion to help others succeed have made him a sought-after speaker and counselor. Jeremy serves as the vice president for Outreach at The Voice of the Martyrs, a global nonprofit that supports persecuted Christians. Previously, Jeremy was the director of Communications for the Museum of the Bible and the executive director of University Relations and Communications for Oral Roberts University in Tulsa, Oklahoma. Jeremy was named PR Professional of the Year by PRSA Tulsa in 2009 and one of the *Tulsa Business Journal*'s Top 40 Under 40 in 2008. Jeremy became a world record holder when ORU broke the Guinness World Record for the most people popping bubble wrap in 2015.

Fred Cook, Fellow PRSA

Fred Cook has worked at Golin for over 35 years. During which, Cook has had the privilege to work with a variety of high-profile CEOs, including Herb Kelleher, Jeff Bezos, and Steve Jobs. He has also managed a wide scope of crises for his clients, including airline crashes, product recalls, and sexual harassment. In 2014, Cook published "Improvise – Unconventional Career Advice from an Unlikely CEO," which shares the wisdom he gained as a cabin boy on a Norwegian tanker, doorman at a 5-star hotel, and chauffeur for drunks. In 2015, after speaking on college campuses around the world, Fred accepted an additional position with the University of Southern California as the director of the USC Center for Public Relations at the Annenberg School, whose mission is to shape the future of public relations and those who will lead it – through research, education, and thought leadership.

Ron Culp, Fellow PRSA

Professional in Residence, Public Relations, and Advertising, DePaul University

Ron Culp is a veteran public relations executive whose career includes senior roles in government, corporations, agencies, and academia. Before joining DePaul University in 2010 as professional in residence, Ron was a managing director of two major agencies, Ketchum and Sard Verbinnen. Prior to his agency career, he was a corporate officer and chief communications officer at Sears. Earlier in his corporate career, Ron held senior corporate communications roles at Sara Lee Corporation, Pitney Bowes, and Eli Lilly. He began his career as a newspaper reporter at The Columbus (Ind.). In addition to co-editing *Mastering Business: C-suite Insights from Strategic Communications Leaders*, Ron is the co-author of *Business Essentials for Strategic Communicators* and *Business Acumen for Strategic Communicators*. In 2019, he organized and edited three editions of *The New Rules of Crisis Management*. For the past 13 years, Ron has been writing the popular PR career blog, Culpwrit.

Anthony D'Angelo, APR, Fellow PRSA

Anthony D'Angelo, APR, Fellow PRSA, joined Syracuse University's Newhouse School of Public Communications as a professor of practice in public relations in August 2015. In 2016, he was named director of Newhouse's Master's Program in Communications Management, and of its Financial and Investor Communications Emphasis. His career has included leadership roles in the corporate, agency, and not-for-profit sectors, including ITT Corporation, the St. Joseph's Hospital Foundation, Magna International, United Technologies, and Sage Marketing Communications. His writing has been featured in *The New York Times*, *Business-Week*, the *Financial Times*, and *USA Today*, and he was a contributor to *The Wall Street Journal*'s "Crisis of the Week" column. He was editor of *75 Years of Impact and Influence: People, Places and Moments in Public Relations History*. D'Angelo served as co-chair of the Commission on Public Relations Education (CPRE) from 2020 to 2021 and was PRSA's national chair in 2018. He received the Newhouse School's Excellence in Teaching Award in 2023.

Kelly Jackson Davis, MMC, APR, Fellow PRSA

Kelly Jackson Davis, MMC, APR, Fellow PRSA, is a senior instructor of public relations in the University of South Carolina School of Journalism and

Mass Communications. A graduate of Furman University, Davis spent more than twenty years in public relations practice in the corporate, government, nonprofit, and agency sectors during which she developed expertise in strategic communications planning, brand development, issues management, and grassroots advocacy. A 2020 inductee into the PRSA College of Fellows, Davis has been recognized for her work and her contributions to the public relations profession with more than sixty professional, peer-reviewed awards. The South Carolina Chapter of the Public Relations Society of America named her the W. Thomas Duke Distinguished Public Relations Practitioner of the Year in 2007. The USC School of Journalism and Mass Communications, from which she holds a Master of Mass Communications degree, selected her as one of its distinguished alumni in 2015.

Mark Dvorak, M.A., APR, Fellow PRSA

By the end of the first day of his first public relations course in college, Mark Dvorak was hooked. In the three decades since, Mark has consistently been drawn to opportunities where powerful communications can transform people and communities. Today, he divides his time between Golin and his own developing consultancy, Mark Dvorak & Co., and his passion project is driving adoption of the early introduction of peanut foods to prevent allergy development. A career-long PRSA member, Mark chairs the Board of Ethics and Professional Standards. He contributed to the creation of Voices4Everyone, served on the Universal Accreditation Board, and co-chaired ICON in 2015. He is a past president of his home Georgia Chapter and a member of its Order of the Phoenix.

Jane Dvorak, APR, Fellow PRSA

Jane Dvorak, APR, Fellow PRSA, started JKD & Company in 1989 and has driven strategic communications programs in industries ranging from healthcare and engineering to agriculture and education with energy, creativity, and impact. Jane is a lifelong learner and leader, an accredited member of PRSA, served as the 2017 PRSA National Chair, and was inducted into the College of Fellows in 2010. She is a two-time Silver Anvil winner among other awards and was named to the Colorado State University Journalism Department Hall of Fame in 2016. She's been an independent practitioner for 35 years and considers her 13-stair journey to JKD headquarters a perfect commute. You can join the #CJRevolution, Jane's personal hashtag, promoting laughter and living fully by connecting with Jane via Twitter/Instagram @Jkdjane, LinkedIn, or on JKD & Company's Facebook page.

Michelle Egan, APR, Fellow PRSA

For three decades, Michelle Egan, APR, Fellow PRSA, has applied her strategic communication skills to advance the reputations of government, nonprofit, and private sector organizations. As a chief communications officer, Egan directs internal and external communications for an oil pipeline company. She is responsible for all aspects of formal company stakeholder, media and government relations, crisis communication, and philanthropy. She supervises an award-winning staff and serves as a member of the Crisis Management Team during critical incidents. Accredited in 2001, Egan has volunteered with PRSA for more than 20 years. She joined the PRSA Board of Directors in 2018, served two terms as Treasurer, and is the 2023 Chair. Her passion for the community runs deep as she volunteers her time with Special Olympics and Catholic Social Services. Egan is a graduate of Boston College and has a master's degree in strategic communication from Seton Hall University.

Geri Ann Evans, MA, APR, Fellow PRSA, President/CEO, Evans PR Group

Geri Ann Evans, APR, is an experienced public relations professional, public speaker, writer, consultant, and educator. In 2003, she opened her own PR firm specializing in helping leadership teams tell more powerful stories. Prior to this, she was VP of Communications for the Florida Hospital Association and the director of public relations for a boutique hotel chain in Orlando, and taught communications for 26 years. She has been published nationally and often presents professional seminars across the nation. A 2014 selectee of the College of Fellows, she served as Chair in 2019. She also served on the national Public Relations Society of America Board for three years. Simultaneously, she served as an advisor to the PRSSA national board. A former officer of the PRSA Sunshine District and former President of the Orlando Chapter, Geri has immersed herself in the profession she loves. Geri holds a B.S. in both English and Speech and an M.A. in Communications.

Gayle Lynn Falkenthal, APR, Fellow PRSA

Gayle Lynn Falkenthal, APR, Fellow PRSA, is the owner of Falcon Valley Group, a San Diego–based strategic communications consulting practice. Her clients include a range of nonprofit, public agency, and business clients. Falkenthal spent 15 years as an award-winning broadcaster and producer before transitioning into a public relations career. Falkenthal applied her skills in increasingly responsible roles, including Director of Public Affairs for the San Diego County District Attorney and Disaster Public Affairs Officer for the American Red Cross prior to starting her practice. Falkenthal is known for her exceptional expertise in crisis communications, as a steady hand and trusted advisor under the most challenging circumstances. She is a skilled strategist, teacher, and collaborator who delivers distinctive messages with a defined call to action supporting her clients' business and organization objectives. Clients single out her talents as a community collaborator, a nimble deadline-driven writer, and an exceptional client partner.

Bob Frause, APR, Fellow PRSA, CEO, Frause

Bob Frause, APR, Fellow PRSA, has provided communications and marketing counsel to clients throughout the United States for more than 50 years. From the early days of his career at Hill and Knowlton and DDB to founder and CEO of The Frause Group, Bob has served hundreds of private, public, and nonprofit sector clients. In addition to his many civic activities, Bob has been involved with the Public Relations Society of America for many years, including positions as 2008 chairman of the College of Fellows, former chairman of the Board of Ethics and Professional Standards, and member of the Society's National Board of Directors. Bob holds a BA in Journalism from Seattle University. Prior to beginning his public relations career, Bob served as a U.S. Army officer, rising to the rank of Captain. He served from 2011 to 2014 as Global Chairman of PROI Worldwide, the profession's largest global network of independent PR agencies.

Amiso M. George, Ph.D., APR, Fellow PRSA

Dr. Amiso M. George, APR, Fellow PRSA, is chair of the Race and Reconciliation Initiative. She is professor and former chair of Strategic Communication Department at Texas Christian University, Fort Worth. A Fulbright scholar (Kyrgyzstan, 2022), she was named the "2017 PRSA Educator of the Year." She received the 2017 Bridge Award for Excellence in Strategic Communication Research from the International Crisis and Risk Communication Conference (ICRCC). George directed the Public Relations program at the University of Nevada, Reno, where she taught the first crisis communication course. A visiting professor at Swinburne University in Australia, she has worked as a crisis consultant in the United States, Asia, and Africa, and has been quoted many times on crisis communication cases in the media. She is co-editor of three books, including *Case Studies in Crisis Communication: International Perspectives* and *Culture and Crisis Communication*. Connect with her on LinkedIn and Twitter @amisogrg

Gene Hall, APR, Fellow PRSA

Gene Hall is the retired Director of Communications for the Texas Farm Bureau, Texas largest organization of farm, ranch, and rural families. Hall served as director for 29 of his 42 years in Farm Bureau Communications. He was responsible for media relations, organizational publications, the TFB printing plant, radio, video, Internet, video, and member communications. He helped launched the TFB video effort in 1978 and, as director, planned and supervised the organization's launch of the website and digital communications. Hall was a pioneer in agricultural advocacy and continues that work as a volunteer today. Nationally recognized as a writer, blogger, and public speaker, Hall is an APR and PRSA Fellow. He writes as a contributor for the Waco Tribune-Herald, does some consulting work, and is a community volunteer. He has been an officer and board member of Waco Kiwanis for three decades and is currently president of the Waco Kiwanis Foundation.

Ken Hagihara, APR, Fellow PRSA

Ken Hagihara is president of Integrity Public Relations, a technology public relations agency. A full-time lecturer at California State University, Fullerton, he teaches public relations writing and campaign courses, manages the student-run agency, and serves as faculty adviser for the PRSSA chapter. He also serves as PRSSA National Faculty Adviser, member of the Universal Accreditation Board, and board member for Pacific Battleship Center. Hagihara retired from the military at the rank of lieutenant commander following a 24-year active-duty and reserve career in the Air Force and Navy that culminated as a Navy public affairs officer. Prior to launching his agency in 2000, Hagihara served as a senior public information representative for the University of California, Irvine, and senior account executive at a technology public relations agency. Hagihara received his bachelor's degree in communications from California State University, Fullerton, and his master's in communication management from University of Southern California.

Margaret Ann Hennen, APR, Fellow PRSA

President, Hennen Communication, LLC

Margaret Ann Hennen is a public relations professional with 40 years of experience in Minnesota business communities. She delivers desired results for corporate and community organizations. An organized, strategic leader with a reputation for motivating individuals and groups, Margaret Ann helps seemingly unrelated entities find common ground and aligns employees, customers, and programs to business goals, helping to achieve strategic results. An active member of PRSA, she is a former Minnesota chapter president and ethics officer. She served on the national PRSA board of directors, the College of Fellows executive committee, and the Board of Ethics and Professional Standards. The 2019 recipient of the Patrick Jackson Award for service to PRSA, she is accredited and is a member of its prestigious College of Fellows. She served as 2022 Chair of the PRSA College of Fellows.

Dean Kruckeberg, Ph.D., APR, Fellow PRSA

Dr. Dean Kruckeberg, APR, Fellow PRSA, is a professor in the Department of Communication Studies at the University of North Carolina at Charlotte.

He is co-author of the books *Public Relations and Community*; *This Is PR*; and *Transparency, Public Relations, and the Mass Media*. He is co-editor of the books *Strategic Communications in Russia* and *Public Relations in the Gulf Cooperation Council Countries*. Dr. Kruckeberg is co-author of the United Arab Emirates textbooks *Principles of Public Relations and of Case Studies in Public Relations*. He has been presented the NCA Public Relations Division Lifetime Achievement Award for Contributions in Public Relations Education, the PRSA Atlas Award for Lifetime Achievement in International Public Relations, the PRSA national "Outstanding Educator" Award, the Jackson Jackson & Wagner Behavioral Research Prize, and the IPR Pathfinder Award. Dr. Kruckeberg was the 2021 recipient of the PRSA Gold Anvil Award. He was co-chair of the Commission on Public Relations Education for 15 years.

Blake Lewis, APR, Fellow PRSA

Blake Lewis is founding principal and chief operating officer of Dallas-based Three Box Strategic Communications, specializing in crisis communications, thought leadership, community relations, and strategic counsel. Prior to founding Three Box predecessor Lewis Public Relations, Blake was a member of the global corporate communications team for EDS (now Hewlett Packard Enterprise) and held senior-level roles at Edelman, the American Heart Association, a regional medical center, and a boutique advertising and public relations firm in the Midwest. Blake earned a Bachelor of Science in Telecommunicative Arts with a minor in sociology and counseling and elective studies in electrical engineering and physics from Iowa State University. He is an accredited member of the Public Relations Society of America (PRSA) and was inducted into the Society's College of Fellows in 2005. Blake is a past national treasurer, national secretary, and board member of PRSA and a former chair of the Universal Accreditation Board.

Kena Lewis, APR, Fellow PRSA

Kena Lewis, APR, Fellow PRSA, is a seasoned communications professional with a diverse background in news, public affairs, marketing, and public relations. She is currently the assistant vice president of Public Affairs and Media Relations for Orlando Health, a not-for-profit healthcare organization with $9.2 billion of assets under management that serves the southeastern United States and Puerto Rico. In that role, Mrs. Lewis directs the healthcare system's public affairs and media relations team and provides lead support on issues management and crisis communications. Mrs. Lewis holds a Bachelor of Arts degree in Communications from the University of Missouri-Columbia and a Master of Arts degree in Communications with an emphasis on Mass Communication from the University of Central Florida. You can find her on Twitter @KenaLewis.

James E. Lukaszewski, ABC, Fellow IABC, APR, Fellow PRSA, PRSA BEPS Emeritus

James E. Lukaszewski (lew-ca-chev-ski) is a well-known writer, author, teacher, scholar, and lecturer in American Public Relations. A Minnesota native whose PR career began in 1974 in the press office of former Minnesota Governor Wendell R. Anderson and as the deputy commissioner of the MN Department of Economic Development. After government, Jim and his wife Barbara opened their first PR firm in Minneapolis in 1978, then from New York in 1986. He has had clients, lectured, or taught in every U.S. state, Canada, Central and South America, Europe, and the Caribbean. Jim worked at senior levels, on the toughest organizational and leadership problems. He authored fourteen books, e-books, manuals, and hundreds of articles. He was an adjunct professor of communication at New York University and a civilian advisor to the U.S. Marine Corps for more than 20 years. He served for 30+ years on the PRSA Board of Ethics and Professional Standards.

Mark McClennan, APR, Fellow PRSA

Mark McClennan, APR, Fellow PRSA, is the general manager of the Boston office of C+C, a communications agency that helps good causes and purpose-driven brands. He was the 2016 National Chair of PRSA and also teaches PR ethics at Boston University. He hosts a weekly blog and podcast, EthicalVoices.com, a weekly blog, and podcast, on ethics and communication. It profiles a communications professional and one key ethical decision or challenge they faced in their career. His book, "Ethical Voices – Practicing Public Relations with Integrity," was released in 2022 by Business Expert Press and quickly become the #1 PR book on Amazon. It includes more than 100 real-world ethics incidents with advice from global industry leaders at companies including Starbucks, Lenovo, the TSA, the Federal Reserve, Harvard Business School, IBM, CDC, and the world's largest public relations agencies.

Mike McDougall, APR, Fellow PRSA, FAAO

President & Founder

Mike McDougall, APR, Fellow PRSA, FAAO, has provided communications and public affairs counsel to some of the world's most prominent organizations for three decades. In 2011, he founded McDougall Communications (mcdougallpr.com), which works with clients on six continents. He previously served as global vice president of Corporate Communications & Public Affairs for Bausch & Lomb and as worldwide director of product and service public relations for Eastman Kodak Company's US$9 billion consumer division. A leader whose techniques are at the heart of the profession's evolution, Mike has garnered prominent international recognition, including 22 Public Relations Society of America Silver Anvils and Awards of Excellence. His high-performing teams have been named *PR Week's* Boutique Agency of the Year and a Corporate Team of the Year finalist. He is a frequent conference speaker and university guest lecturer. He resides in suburban Rochester, N.Y.

Debra A. Miller, APR Fellow PRSA

Dr. Debra A. Miller, APR Fellow PRSA, an award-winning leader in strategic communications and public relations management, is the director of Communications for Cone Health, the preeminent healthcare system in the Piedmont Triad section of North Carolina. Dr. Miller has 40+ years of experience working in several industries, including financial services, higher education, professional services, and federal and municipal agencies. She is the first African American Chair of PRSA and a Gold Anvil winner.

Renea Morris, M.Ed., APR, Fellow PRSA

Renea Morris has been a higher education leader for more than 12 years in a 30-year career in marketing and public relations that also spans the corporate and nonprofit sectors. Her work has been recognized with two Emmy nominations and several industry awards, including PRSA's Silver Anvil Award of Excellence. Morris is a longstanding PRSA member and became a Fellow PRSA in 2021. She serves as the 2023 Chair of PRSA's Counselors to Higher Education section. She earned her Master of Education degree from Ohio University. Originally from Chicago, she earned a bachelor's in communications from the University of Illinois at Chicago and holds a professional designation in Public Relations from UCLA. Morris and her husband, Reginald, have four adult children and enjoy being empty nesters and grandparents.

Mickey G. Nall, APR, Fellow PRSA

International award-winning public relations agency professional Mickey G. Nall, APR, Fellow PRSA, develops, implements, and evaluates communications programs that make a positive difference in the lives of clients' target audiences. Beginning in 2018, Mickey became professional in residence at his alma mater, the University of Florida, following more than 20 years at Ogilvy Public Relations (part of Ogilvy & Mather). He has designed and implemented hundreds of campaigns that move the proverbial needle in consumer and health communications, for such illustrious brands as The Coca-Cola Company, UPS, U.S. Centers for Disease Control and Prevention, Lincoln Motor Company, NFL, and Darden Restaurant Group, to name just a few. Active in the Public Relations Society of America, he is accredited (APR), a PRSA Fellow (2009), and was the 2022 recipient of PRSA's highest individual honor, recognizing lifetime achievement, The Gold Anvil Award.

Colonel Christian Patterson, APR, Fellow PRSA

Colonel Christian Patterson currently serves as commander of the U.S. Army Engineer Research and Development Center, headquartered in Vicksburg, Mississippi. During his 29-year career, the combat and peacekeeping mission veteran has deployed to Bosnia, Kosovo, and Afghanistan. He has also responded to several weather emergencies in Mississippi and completed special assignments in France, Honduras, the Dominican Republic, and St. Kitts and Nevis. Christian received his Accreditation in Public Relations + Military Communication credential, October 3, 2012, from the Public Relations Society of America's Universal Accreditation Board. He also possesses a Master of Business Administration degree from Belhaven University; Bachelor of Arts in Mass Communication degree from Louisiana State University; Associate in Arts in Radio, TV, and Film degree from Hinds Community College; and a Professional Certificate in Strategic Communication and Leadership from Seton Hall University. Christian is currently pursuing a Doctor of Philosophy in Communication degree through Liberty University.

Judith T. Phair, APR, Fellow PRSA

Judith (Judy) T. Phair, APR, Fellow PRSA, is president, PhairAdvantage Communications, LLC, providing counsel primarily for higher education and nonprofit associations. Her career has included vice presidencies, encompassing national and international strategic communications, at the Graduate Management Admission Council (owner of the GMAT exam), Council on Competitiveness, University of Maryland Biotechnology Institute, and Goucher College. She also served as adjunct professor at Goucher and Towson State University and senior advisor for the Council of Independent Colleges. The 2005 PRSA president and CEO is past chair of the PRSA College of Fellows as well as co-chair of the PRSA Educational Affairs Committee and Commission on Public Relations Education (CPRE). Judy received the Gold Anvil, PRSA's highest award, in 2010 and the David Ferguson Award in 2014, and is a member of the PRSA National Capital Chapter Hall of Fame. She received her M.A. from the University of Maryland and B.A. from Simmons University.

Cheryl Procter-Rogers, APR, Fellow PRSA, MCC, MBA, MA

An award-winning PR and business strategist for more than 40 years, Cheryl Procter-Rogers has worked with an impressive portfolio of executives and Fortune 100 companies as an executive for Ernst & Young, DePaul

University, Home Box Office (HBO), Nielsen Marketing Research, and Golden State Mutual. As a consultant, she established her consulting firm in 1986, A Step Ahead, working with a variety of clients across many business sectors, including Coca-Cola, Nissan, Allstate, McDonald's, McCain Foods, Sigma Gamma Rho Sorority, and Magellan Corporation. She served as the 2006 president and CEO of the Public Relations Society of America (PRSA), holds a PRSA credential, is a member of its College of Fellows, and earned the organizations' lifetime achievement award, the Gold Anvil. She served as 2023 vice chair of the Global Enterprise board of the International Coaching Federation and holds its master certified coach credential. Learn more at www.cherylprocterrogers.com.

Bey-Ling Sha, Ph.D., APR, Fellow PRSA

Bey-Ling Sha, Ph.D., APR, Fellow PRSA, is a higher education leader whose work has influenced scholarship, teaching, and practice. Her pioneering research at the intersection of identity, activism, and public relations earned her the 2018 Pathfinder Award from the Institute for Public Relations. Her other honors include the Public Relations Society of America's 2012 Outstanding Educator Award, a 2021 President's Award for her service to the Society of Professional Journalists, the 2022 Bruce K. Berger Educator Mentor Award from the Plank Center for Leadership in Public Relations, and the 2023 Lionel C. Barrow Jr. Award for Distinguished Achievement in Diversity Research and Education, from the Association for Education in Journalism and Mass Communication. Dr. Sha is a past editor-in-chief (2016–2021) of the *Journal of Public Relations Research*, past chair (2014) of the Universal Accreditation Board, and the surviving co-author of the most-recent edition of *Cutlip and Center's Effective Public Relations*.

Stacey Smith, APR, Fellow PRSA

Stacey Smith, APR, Fellow PRSA, is a senior counsel and partner with Jackson Jackson & Wagner. With over 40 years of experience counseling an extensive range of clients, she specializes in applying behavioral strategies and theories to help organizations build strategic and solid relationships with stakeholders. She is co-author of *The Public Relations Practices, Managerial Case Studies and Problems*, and *The Public Relations Firm*. A public speaker as well as teacher, she has presented frequently before numerous national public relations organizations and taught as adjunct faculty at Antioch University New England, New England College, and the University of New Hampshire. Stacey is a member of the Institute for Public Relation's Behavioral Insights Group and Immediate Past Chair of the Commission on Public Relation's Education. Stacey graduated from the University of Tennessee with a B.S. in Communications and earned her graduate degree in Management from Antioch University New England.

Philip Tate, APR, Fellow PRSA

Philip Tate, APR, Fellow PRSA, President of Tate Strategic in Charlotte, North Carolina, is a brand builder and strategic communicator with more than 35 years of experience in public relations, marketing, and advertising. During his tenure as senior vice president for Luquire George Andrews (LGA), he directed award-winning campaigns for many of the agency's leading clients, including National Gypsum, Lincoln Harris, Rodgers Builders, and the Charlotte 49ers. Philip has devoted much of his volunteer time to PRSA. He is past chair of the PRSA College of Fellows and previously served two terms as national treasurer on the PRSA national board of directors. He has also been active with the PRSA Independent Practitioners Alliance, Counselors Academy, and as a member of the Board of Ethics and Professional Standards (BEPS). Philip graduated from Vanderbilt University with a Bachelor of Arts degree in English and a double minor in political science and history.

Ana Toro, APR, Fellow PRSA

Ana Toro is a bilingual and bicultural strategic communications professional, with over 30 years of experience in the industry. Between 1995 and 2002, she managed programs and campaigns for Anheuser-Busch, Chrysler, Coors, Merial Central America & Caribbean, Philip Morris, Royal Caribbean, The Shell Company, Merck, Toyota, and Volvo Car Corporation. In 2005, she began supporting the Centers for Disease Control and Prevention and National Institutes of Health in public affairs and as health equity communications team lead for the COVID-19 response. Prior to joining CDC in 2019, she served in leadership roles at ICF and FleishmanHillard. She is the recipient of over 15 awards and recognitions, including Order of the Phoenix, Georgia Public Relations Hall of Fame, and PRSA College of Fellows. Ana has a bachelor's in Media Writing and master's in Public Relations from the Universidad del Sagrado Corazón in PR, plus a certificate in D&I in the Workplace from USF.

Marisa Vallbona, APR, Fellow PRSA

Marisa Vallbona, APR, Fellow PRSA, is a distinguished public relations professional with a rich history of working with world-renowned companies through her leadership of CIM Inc PR, a firm she founded in 1990. Her expertise spans branding, product launches, business strategy, crisis communications, reputation management, speaker training, media relations, and more. She has won four Silver Anvil Awards (the Oscars of the PR industry) from the Public Relations Society of America (PRSA), including a Best of Show for launching XM Satellite Radio, and has been recognized with a Marquis Lifetime Achievement Award, as well as a "Women Who Mean Business Award" from the San Diego Business Journal, among many other accolades. Her work has also been featured in numerous business books, and she has been quoted in various news media outlets. In addition to CIM Inc PR, Marisa co-founded PRConsultants Group, a national network of PR firms in every major U.S. market and Puerto Rico. She has held numerous community and professional leadership roles, serving PRSA for more than 22 years on the local, regional, and national level. She also served as chair of the Universal Accreditation Board. Marisa is multilingual, fluent in Spanish, and conversant in French. She holds citizenships in the United States, Costa Rica, and Spain.

Rebecca M. Villarreal, APR, Fellow PRSA

Rebecca M. Villarreal, APR, Fellow PRSA, has been a public relations professional since 2000. She has worked primarily in education for K-12 public school districts and higher education. Villarreal joined PRSA in 2005 and served as the San Antonio Chapter President in 2011. She is a Texas School Public Relations Association member and served as President in 2022–2023. Villarreal is a frequent presenter at state conferences and area universities, sharing her expertise in public relations, crisis communication, and media relations. She is active in her community and volunteers her time with several nonprofits to help with publicity efforts and event planning. She earned her Accreditation in Public Relations (APR) in 2017 and was inducted into the PRSA College of Fellows in 2022. She and her husband reside in Texas with their three children. Her goal in life is to leave the world better than she found it.

Dennis Wilcox, Ph.D., APR, Fellow PRSA

Dr. Dennis L. Wilcox, APR, is professor emeritus of public relations and former director of the School of Journalism and Mass Communications at San Jose State University in California. Dr. Wilcox is the author of several major textbooks: *Public Relations Strategies and Tactics* (12E), *Public Relations Writing and Media Techniques* (8E), and *Think: Public Relations* (2E). He is former chair of the public relations division of AEJMC and the PRSA Educator's Academy, and served on the PRSA board of directors. His honors include PRSA's Outstanding Educator Award, the Xifra-Heras Award from the University of Girona in Spain, an award for excellence from the Public Relations Society of India, and an honorary doctorate from the University of Bucharest. In addition to being a Fulbright professor at the University of Botswana, Dr. Wilcox has been a visiting professor at Chulalongkorn University in Thailand, Queensland University of Technology in Australia, and Rhodes University in South Africa.

Olga Mayoral Wilson, APR, Fellow PRSA

Olga Mayoral Wilson is a proven strategic crisis communicator and leader who advocates for PR ethics and diversity, equity, and inclusion (DEI) initiatives. As an educator and faculty member, she continues to mentor and support students and young professionals. 2020–2021–2022 included involvement in the PRSA College of Fellows Executive Committee as 2020 Treasurer-Secretary, as 2021 Vice Chair and Induction Committee Chair, and 2022 Induction Committee. Olga continues advising nonprofits: San Antonio Area Foundation (SAAF) Committee on Aging and Scholarships, PRSA 75th Anniversary Committee, PRSA National DEI Committee member, PRSA Mentor-Mentee Program, PRSA Foundation Scholarships, PRSA-SA Chapter (APR Program), PRSSA Bateman Competition, and PRSA College of Fellows *GoodFellows*, among others. Her contributions include *PR Strategist* and *Strive*; as guest speaker at ARPPR's 50th Anniversary (Puerto Rico's Public Relations Assoc.), workshops sponsored by the Global Alliance for DEI Month Dialogue ('23), and the NLCUP (National Assoc. Latino Credit Unions & Professionals) and the AACUC (African American Credit Unions Coalition) "Commitment to Change" Webinar Series Panel ('20).

Ira W. Yellen, APR, Fellow PRSA

A graduate from Pratt Institute, 1969, Ira W. Yellen started as an urban residential designer in Brooklyn, NY. While interacting with noted anthropologist Margaret Mead, he explored the relationships that intertwined commerce, civic institutions, society, and human nature where communication was a key for engaging various constituents – a perspective he practices today. This led him to learn how to incorporate public relations, marketing, and visual language for creating positive outcomes for his clients. For over 40 years, he has led through his firm, *Tall Timbers Marketing*, formerly First Experience Communications, a wide range of projects that provide strategic counsel and tactical support for educational institutions, healthcare organizations, government public policy issues, and emerging technology companies. He was a chronicler and fundraiser for the Statue of Liberty/Ellis Island Centennial restoration projects between 1983 and 1986, raising more than $100,000 for creating, publishing, and distributing an educational supplementary curriculum for public schools across the nation. This was one of his proudest accomplishments that honored his and other family's immigrant experience.

Index

Note: Page numbers in *italics* indicate a figure, and page numbers in **bold** indicate a table on the corresponding page.

Accreditation in Public Relations (APR) **13**, 78, 87, 106, 110–124
Accrediting Council on Education in Journalism and Mass Communications (ACEJMC) 102
acculturative stress 26, 30–31
achieved identity 26, 33
achievement/responsibility 3, 4
adaptive capacity 6, 20, 47
adaptive self-reflection 57
advocates, role of 78–81
agency, category of 3–4
anchoring event 3, 16, 36
Arnold, J.W. 12, **13**, 16, 110
Arthur W. Page Center 110
ascribed cultural identity 25
ascribed identity 25, 28–29
avowed identity 25

Baby Boomers 11
Barber, Mary Deming **13**, 66–67, 78–79, 97–98, 102
Barkelew, Ann H. 11, *12*, **13**, 18, 43, 45, 75, 79, 110
Baylor University Institute for Oral History 1
bicultural stress 27
Bradley University Black Alumni Alliance 30
Burfeind, Barbara A. **13**, 43, 48, 78, 111

burnout 61–64
Burton, Jeremy C. **13**, 39, 43, 61, 66, 111

California Commission for Improving Life Through Service 89
career setbacks: experiences 41–43; negative feedback from colleagues 42
childhood challenges 19
civility 74
Civil Rights era 18–19
collaboration 77–78
Commission on Public Relations Education 102, 106, 112, 117, 120
communion 3, 4, 14, 73; theme of care/help 88–89
compounded adversities 2
concentration of effect 95
connection to others 33
consequentialism 86
consistency 33, 41
Cook, Fred 5, *6*, 49, 52, 111–112
coping strategies 27, 33
crises: communication 44; as crucibles 43–49; encounter or identity 2; managing 43–49, 61
critical reflection 4–5; adaptive self-reflection 57; challenges 64; disappointment 60–61; failures

and regrets 60–61, 67–68; health and wellness issues 62–63; maladaptive 57; managing crisis 61; negative feelings 65; overwork and burnout 61–64; patience and resilience 65; people pleasing 58; personal reflection, six-step process for engaging in 68; personal struggles 64–67; physical and mental exhaustion 62; potential barriers 57; prosocial silence 58; resilience 61; risks 59–60; self-affirmation approaches 57; volunteering, limitations 63–64
crucibles: compounded adversities 2; creation of narrative 1; crises as crucibles 43–49; critical reflection 4–5; encounter or identity crisis 2; engaging in unbiased processing 4, 5; ethical role models, concept of 8; experiences model *27*; idealistic childhoods of leaders 4–5; importance of studying 1–2; in leader development 4–9; leader development, definition 4; leadership proficiencies and virtues 6–7; narratives 9; new territory 1–2, 49–54; practical wisdom 8–9; primary categories 1–2; public relations leadership 7; resilience 73–74; suspension 2, 54–56; "trial by fire" experiences 91–94; virtue or habitus, definition 8
Culp, Ron **13**, 43, 46, 58, 75, 82, 89, 104, 112
cultural differences, awareness 25–26
cultural identity 11, 25–27, 32–33, 105

D'Angelo, Anthony **13**, 22, 60–61, 74, 77, 112
Davis, Kelly Jackson 8, **13**, 49, 53, 76, 112–113

desire for control 64
disappointment 41, 42, 60–61, 67, 68
Dvorak, Jane **13**, 22, 113
Dvorak, Mark **13**, 58, 65–66, 90, 113

early leadership 14–19; childhood challenges 19; Civil Rights movement 18–19; experiences as anchoring events 16–17; familial and memorable experiences 16–19; originating event 14–15; ROTC program and memorable message 16; volunteer service 17–18
Egan, Michelle 7, **13**, 85–87, 91, 94–95, 113–114
emotions 2–3, 19, 26–27, 30, 39, 43, 53, 77, 108
empathy or kindness 4, 6, 19, 74, 96
empowerment 3, 4, 12
encounter or identity crisis 2, 25
ethical dilemmas 85–86, 92–93, 95, 106
ethical leadership: APR 87; choices for public relations leaders 94; communion theme of care/ help 88–89; consequentialism 86; demonstrating 91–94; development of 105–106; ethical dilemmas 95; ethics competencies or abilities 86–87; ethics of care 89; expense reporting 89–90; experiences 90–91; factors, moral intensity 94–96; moral courage 86–88, 92–93; PRSA code of ethics 93; role as an ethics counselor 92; steps, caring 89; "trial by fire" experiences 91–94; values and virtues 96–98; virtue ethics 86
ethical role models 8, 104–105
ethics competencies or abilities 86–87, 106, 108
ethics counselor 92
ethics of care 89
eudaimonia or human flourishing 70

European Communication Monitor 2022 report 61
Evans, Geri A. **13**, 17, 63–64, 68, 114
exhaustion 62
expense reporting 89–90
experiences 90–91; as anchoring events 16–17; familial and memorable 16–19; "trial by fire" 91–94

factors, moral intensity 94–96
failures 60–61, 67–68
fairness/justice 20
Falkenthal, Gayle Lynn **13**, 43–44, 62, 73, 114–115
Fellows as mentors 82–83
Frause, Bob **13**, 16, 85, 87–89, 115
future research and life projects: activities 101; advice for young professionals 106–107; beliefs 102; blogs on public relations careers 104; development of ethical leaders 105–106; ethical role models 104–105; inspirational videos and stories 104; podcast, "Ethical Voices" 103–104; research 107–108; service with DE&I committees 103; truth and agricultural issues 103; values 102–103

Generation X 11
generosity 71–73; communion 73; importance of 71; making an impact 71–72
George, Amiso M. **13**, 21, 42, 71, 115
grief 64

habitus, definition 8
Hagihara, Kenneth T. **13**, 19, 116
Hall, Gene 14, 39, 59, 103, 115–116
health issues 62–63
Hennen, Margaret Ann **13**, 32, 38–39, 72, *72*, 77–78, 93, 116
honesty 74, 86, 91, 96

idealistic childhoods of leaders 4–5
identity: acculturative stress 26, 30–31; achieved identity 26, 33; ascribed cultural identity 25; ascribed identity 25, 28; avowed identity 25; bilingual fluency and social connections 26; coping strategies 27; crucible experiences model *27*; cultural differences, awareness 25–26; definition 25; emotions 26; identity search 26–27; intersectionality 28; majority identity model 31–32; motivations 33; personal advocacy 33–34; resilience 27; social connectedness 33; subjugated ascriptions 29; unexamined cultural identity 26; unexamined identity or pre-encounter phase 32
inclusion 18, 33, 74
intersectionality 28
isolation, cultural/social 27
The Itasca Symposium: The Architecture of Professional Progression 11

Jesuit education 85

Kruckeberg, Dean A. **13**, 42–43, 61, 116–117

leader characteristics: adaptive capacity 20; among Fellows 20; care and desire to develop others 20–21, *21*; exhibited by exemplars 20–21; personal growth 22–23; positivity 21–22; vices 22–23
leader development: crucibles in 4–9; definition 4; description 4; impact of crucibles on *6*
Lewis, Blake D. **13**, 22, 30, 43, 54, 75, 78, 96, 101, 117
Lewis, Kena 19, 30, *31*, 43, 47, 60, 117

life-altering crucible experiences 36
lifetime achievement award 12–13
listening, importance of 1, 75–76
Lukaszewski, James E. 13, 41, 118

magnitude of consequences 94–95
majority identity model 31–32;
   acceptance 32; resistance 32
maladaptive, reflection 57
Mayoral-Wilson, Olga 13, 29, 92,
   103, 124
McClennan, Mark W. 13, 40, 62,
   103, 118
McDougall, Michael L. 13, 95,
   118–119
memorable message 39, 74
memories 3, 16, 26, 39, 90
mentors/mentoring 78–81;
   instrumental support, roles
   of 79; psychosocial support
   79; reciprocal nature of social
   influence, concept of 78–81
Miller, Debra A. 13, 49–50, 51, *51*,
   71, 76, 119
moral courage 92–93; examples
   86–88
moral efficacy 86
moral exemplars 8, 14, 87; selection 14
moral intensity 94–95
moral vision/development 70–71
Morris, Renea 13, 33, 88–89, 119
mortality, confronting: anchoring
   event 36; life-altering crucible
   experiences 3, 36; memorable
   message 39; resilience 39;
   resiliency 41; transformative
   experiences 36
motivation 3–4, 15, 33, 73, 101, 104

Nall, Mickey G. 13, 41–42, 58–59,
   81–82, 119–120
narratives 1, 4, 9, 14, 73, 89, 108
negative feelings 2, 39, 64–65
neoteny 20
new territory 1–2; crucibles 49–54;
   perseverance and determination
   53; student and donor relations 50;
   unconventional career paths 52–53

observation, learning through 81–82
optimism 20
originating event 14–15
Outstanding Educator Award 42

Patterson, Colonel Christian 13,
   20–21, 64–65, 74, 96–97,
   102, 120
perfectionism 64, 96
personal advocacy 33–34
personal reflection, six-step process
   for engaging in 68
Phair, Judith T. 13, *49*, 49–50,
   102, 120
phronesis 8–9, 70, 83, 105–106;
   advice on speaking up 76–77;
   civility 74; fellows as mentors
   82–83; generosity 71–73;
   honesty 74; learning through
   observation 81–82; listening,
   importance of 76; memorable
   message 74; mentors and
   advocates, role of 78–81; moral
   vision/development 70–71;
   power of listening 75–76;
   primary socialization 70;
   resilience 70, 73–74; sacrifice
   75; secondary socialization 70;
   social norms 70; speaking up
   and contributing, importance
   of 76–77; teamwork and
   collaboration 77–78; wisdom 70,
   81–82
podcast, "Ethical Voices" 103–104
positivity 20–22
practical wisdom *see* phronesis
predictability 33
primary socialization 70–71
probability of effect 95
Procter-Rogers, Cheryl 13, 16–17,
   29–30, *30*, 54, 120–121
prosocial silence 58
public relations leadership 7, 94
Public Relations Society of America
   (PRSA) 7, 11; code of ethics 93;
   College of Fellows 8; historic
   election as national chair 51;
   national chair of *30*

racial discrimination 11, 27, 29
resilience 27, 39, 61, 65, 70, 73–74,
    96; and approaches 2; definition
    2, 27, 73–74; leadership skills,
    through crucibles 73–74
resiliency 2, 41
ROTC program 6, 14, 16

sacrifice 75
secondary socialization 70
security 33, 63
self-affirmation approaches 57
self-confidence 64, 68
service with DE&I committees 103
Sha, Bey-Ling **13**, 25, 33, 102, 121
shared life, principles of 70
Silent Generation 11
Smith, Stacey **13**, *80*, 80–81,
    121–122
social connectedness 33
social consensus 95
social norms 70
speaking up, importance of 76–77
studying, importance of 1–2
subjugated ascriptions 29
suspension 2; crucibles and starting
    own businesses 54–56; moment
    54–55

Task Force on Professionalism 11
Tate, Philip 8, **13**, 15–16, 32,
    40–41, 60, 63, 93, 98, 122
teamwork 77–78
Three Box Strategic
    Communications 75

time management 95
Toro, Ana **13**, 28, 33, 41, 103, 122
transformative experiences 36
"trial by fire" experiences 91–94

unbiased processing 5
unconventional career paths
    52–53
unexamined cultural identity 26–27
unexamined identity or pre-
    encounter phase 31–32

Vallbona, Marisa **13**, 26–27, 36, *37*,
    55, 104, 122–123
values 102–103; core principles
    and values 97; description 96;
    personality inventory of PRSA
    Fellows 96; questions for public
    relations professionals 98
vices 17, 22–23, 108
Villarreal, Rebecca M. **13**, 28, 67,
    92, 123
virtues: definition 8; ethics 86;
    of love and kindness 97–98;
    personal virtue as caring 96–97
Voices4Everyone initiative 74
volunteering, limitations 63–64
volunteer service 17–18, 101

Wilcox, Dennis L. **13**, 18–19, 123
wisdom 1, 3–4, 70, 81–82; practical
    8–9, 70, 83, 105–106

Yellen, Ira W. **13**, 62–63, 124
Youth Job Awareness Project 88

Printed in the United States
by Baker & Taylor Publisher Services